# FOLK

# DANCING

........................................

A GUIDE FOR SCHOOLS,

COLLEGES, AND

RECREATION GROUPS

*THE MACMILLAN COMPANY*

First Printing

Library of Congress catalog card number: 62-7377

The Macmillan Company, New York
Brett-Macmillan Ltd., Galt, Ontario

Printed in the United States of America

# Folk Dancing

# Richard Kraus

Professor of Education, Department of

Health Education, Physical Education

and Recreation, Teachers College,

Columbia University

ILLUSTRATED BY THE AUTHOR

*NEW YORK*

to Mrs. Siller and Fred Schwartz

who made the music for our dancing

# Preface

......................................................

FOLK DANCING offers a varied collection of European and American folk dances, including many which have been used for years in school physical education and community recreation programs—plus a good number of dances which have been more recently presented. In addition, six chapters have been designed to provide leaders and teachers with a knowledge of the background of folk dancing, a thorough analysis of fundamental movements and step patterns, and effective teaching methods.

Over fifty illustrations, many of them showing traditional folk costumes, make the actions come alive. To further enrich the book, listings of folk dance schools and camps, stores that specialize in folk dance records, and other folk dance books have been included.

Thus, *Folk Dancing* is intended both as a valuable handbook for teachers and leaders and as a handy collection of popular folk dances for those who enjoy folk dancing as personal recreation. Since excellent records are available for each of the dances described, and since it is no longer the practice to have piano accompanists in most school and college classes—musical notation is not provided for the dances. However, a measure-for-measure analysis accompanies the description of the dance action in every case. Miss Mary Ikeda, who assisted the author in preparing these breakdowns, points out that the designation of sections of music as "A," "B," etc., is in some cases arbitrary, since there is not always a radical change in the melody. Nonetheless, dividing the music into sections in this way will be helpful to the teacher who must work out the action for himself from the description. In any case, as Chapter Four points out, it is necessary for the teacher to thoroughly familiarize himself with the dance action, working it out with the record, before actually teaching it to a class.

The author wishes to express his gratitude to Prof. Mildred Spiesman of Queens College, who provided a perceptive and authoritative critical analysis of the manuscript—and also to his many students in folk dance classes at Columbia University and in community recreation groups. It is not an idle comment to say that he learned more from his students than they learned from him.

(Note: Within the diagrams appearing in the text—

▷ indicates man facing toward right of page;
▷ indicates woman facing toward right of page.)

And now—good dancing!

RICHARD KRAUS

*Teachers College,*
*Columbia University*

# Contents

1    THE ''WHAT'' AND ''WHY'' OF FOLK
DANCING     1

2    FUNDAMENTAL POSITIONS,
FORMATIONS, AND SKILLS     9

3    BASIC FOLK DANCE STEPS     21

4    FOLK DANCE TEACHING GUIDES     33

5    PLANNING FOLK DANCE INSTRUCTION
UNITS     42

6    EASY FOLK DANCES FOR ELEMENTARY
GRADES     54

7    CIRCLE DANCES WITHOUT PARTNERS     76

8    COUPLE DANCES     89

9    ATTACHED COUPLE DANCES     116

10    PARTNER-CHANGING DANCES     134

11    DANCES FOR THREE     150

*12* LONGWAYS DANCES 161

*13* DANCES IN THE SQUARE FORMATION 185

*14* FOLK FESTIVALS AND SPECIAL
EVENTS 202

APPENDIX:

List of Dances 209
Folk Dance Costumes 214
Folk Dance Camps and Summer Schools 216
Bibliography of Useful Books 217
Sources for Folk Dance Records 221

# Folk Dancing

# The "What" and "Why" of Folk Dancing

......................................... *1*

*JUST WHAT IS* folk dancing—and *why* is it such an important and enjoyable part of school and college physical education and community recreation programs?

The term is generally used to describe the traditional recreational dance forms of the common people. Most folk dances are of anonymous origin and have been handed down from generation to generation over a considerable period of time. Centuries ago, they were closely related to the customs, rituals and occupations of the people who performed them; today, however, most folk dances have lost these associations and are performed primarily—in the United States, at least—for social and recreational reasons. Fortunately, the folk backgrounds of many dances are still known and provide a fascinating storehouse of information about the people who originated them.

The reader should be familiar with several other terms which are often used interchangeably, or confused, with folk dancing.

*National dance* refers to the type of folk dance which is

found most widely throughout a given country, often with a number of regional variations. Examples would be the Italian Tarantella, the Hungarian Czardas and the Serbian Kolo. *Character dance*, a term not heard too frequently today, describes those deliberately created dances in which characteristic steps and movements have been fitted to the traditional folk tunes of a nation, often for exhibition purposes. They are not true folk forms, although they give an exciting impression of the folk dances of a people. *Ethnic*, or *ethnological dance* is the kind of dance performed in those cultures or primitive tribes where dance has retained its close kinship with religious ritual and community custom. Ethnic dances tend to require a high level of special performing skill and are rarely done by recreational groups in this country.

Two other related terms are *square dancing* and *American round dancing*. Square dances are simply dances for four couples, done in the quadrille formation; when traditional, they should be considered part of the total folk dance picture. A great number of new square dance movement patterns have recently been created in the United States. Since they cannot be considered true folk dances, they are not dealt with here; to describe them adequately would require a separate book. Round dances are couple dances, either those which were popular in the last century, or which have been composed fairly recently. They are usually based on waltz, two-step, or schottische rhythms, and set to modern tunes. Because many of these dances are catchy and enjoyed by young and old alike, a selected number of the best ones appear in this book.

A final term, *country dancing*, is sometimes used to describe traditional recreational dancing—particularly when it includes the set dances (circle, line, and square) of English origin. The label is somewhat misleading, since people who live both in cities and rural areas enjoy "country" dancing. However, it conveys something of the informal, friendly spirit of these dances.

No matter what words we use to describe it, folk dancing is a unique and valuable form of group activity. It contributes greatly to intercultural understanding, social adjustment, and physical well-being, and it is not surprising that it has become an important part of the physical education and recreation program in American schools, colleges, and communities.

## Folk Dancing in Education

It was recognized centuries ago that dancing in its many forms had much to offer in the upbringing of youth. John Locke wrote:

... since nothing appears to me to give children so much becoming confidence and behavior, and so to raise them to the conversation of those above their age, as dancing, I think they should be taught to dance as soon as they are capable of it.[1]

[1] John Locke, *Some Thoughts Concerning Education*. London, W. Baynes, 1800. p. 60.

Charles W. Eliot, President of Harvard University during the latter part of the nineteeenth century, wrote in a letter to Charles Francis Adams:

I have often said that if I were compelled to have one required subject in Harvard College, I would make it dancing if I could. West Point has been very wise in this respect . . .[2]

In 1904, Dr. Luther Halsey Gulick, a pioneer in the field of American physical education, wrote appreciatively of the desirable effects of folk dancing:

There is slowly but surely coming into our secondary schools and colleges a recognition of dancing as a bodily discipline. I refer . . . to the old folk dancing . . . it is excellent and will enrich the physical training program.[3]

A great contribution to the growth of folk dancing in America's schools was made by Elizabeth Burchenal, founder and first president of the American Folk Dance Society. She wrote several books, did original dance research in many countries, established folk dance playground programs and taught many leaders over a period of several decades. Louis Chalif, founder of the Chalif Russian Normal School of Dancing in New York in 1907, also published widely and organized many courses, institutes, festivals, and folk dance pageants. Others, such as Mary Wood Hinman of Chicago and Sarah Gertrude Knott, director of the annual Folk Festival in St. Louis, stimulated educational interest in folk dancing. Dr. Lloyd Shaw of Colorado was unique for his popularizing of traditional dances of the American West and Southwest among school people during the 1930's and 1940's.

Just what are the important values that folk dancing brings to its participants? They may be described in four categories: physical, social, cultural, and recreational.

*Physical Values.* As a vigorous activity which makes use of a wide variety of body movements, folk dancing contributes to the learning of motor skills, the development of a strong sense of rhythm and spatial relationships, and the improvement of strength, agility, balance, and endurance. Dr. Frederick Rand Rogers, former president of the North American Physical Fitness Institute, has been an especially vocal adherent of dance for its sound physical values. Ideally, however, the folk dance performer does more than exercise a set of muscles; he moves gracefully and expressively, in a fully integrated and coordinated way.

[2] Marks, Joseph, *America Learns to Dance.* New York, Exposition Press, 1957. p. 102.
[3] Gulick, Luther Halsey, *Physical Education by Muscular Exercises.* Philadelphia, P. Blakiston's Son And Company, 1904. p. 63.

*Social Values.* The school or college student who participates in folk dancing learns to cooperate with other members of his group and to accept responsibility for playing his part in the group situation. Through dancing together, children and young people learn consideration for each other and a code of social behavior. Some amusing excerpts may be found in a manual written by an old Philadelphia dancing master:

It is very impolite and insulting in either lady or gentleman while dancing in a quadrille, to mar the pleasure of others by galloping around or inside of the next set . . .

It is very indecorous, and out of place, to give way to immoderate laughing, sneering or commenting at those who are present . . .[4]

While the language is quaint, the ideas are still sound. It is generally recognized today that a certain amount of coeducational social activity helps give teen-age boys and girls (often shy and lacking in confidence beneath their air of assurance) a needed sense of security and a wholesome attitude toward those of the opposite sex. Folk dancing helps to provide this, without any of the overtones of "teen-age rebellion" or sex attraction that are found in the double-entendre lyrics and sophisticated themes of "rock-and-roll" or other forms of ballroom dance music.

Through folk dancing, it is possible for the child to gain a strong sense of "belonging," a feeling of personal worth and achievement, and the knowledge that he is contributing to the pleasure and welfare of others. And, when the group plans a special project, trip, festival, or demonstration, the values of team cooperation become even more pronounced!

*Cultural Values.* Folk dancing is an ideal medium for developing international understanding and respect for those of other cultures. Mary Shambaugh has written:

To some the study of folk dancing is only the silhouette; only the study of movement. To others, the study of folk dancing is a vivid picture of national life with a colorful, fanciful background of folk costume, custom, art, music and legend.[5]

Not only may folk dancing be closely linked with the better understanding of the people of other nations or other historical periods of our own country, through correlation with the social studies; it is also readily combined with the study of music, the languages of other lands, graphic arts, and dramatic activity. Viewed in this light, folk dancing becomes an excellent

[4] Tolman, Beth and Page, Ralph, *The Country Dance Book.* New York, A. S. Barnes, 1937. pp. 44-45.
[5] Shambaugh, Mary, *Folk Festivals.* New York, A. S. Barnes, 1932. p. vii.

means of enlivening and enriching unit studies of all sorts—and often provides the basic theme around which United Nations festivals and One World pageants may be organized.

**Recreational Values.** Not to be overlooked is the "fun" aspect of folk dancing—the sheer pleasure to be gained from lively dancing in a friendly social group. When properly presented, folk dancing can do much to relieve mental strain or emotional tension; whether the dancer is a ten-year-old child or a tired businessman, he should find the experience relaxed and exhilarating, and an easy way to make new friends. *All* forms of dance should provide enjoyable recreation, but too often square and round dance clubs are geared for *couples* with a fairly high level of skill. The beginning folk dancer, however, need not have a partner, since so many of the dances are done in circles, lines, or other formations *without* partners. And, in most large communities, it is fairly easy for him to find a group where he can dance on his own level and be warmly welcomed.

It is true that many children and some adults may view folk dancing with some suspicion at the outset. The teen-ager may refer to it as either "long-hair" or "square." But, once he has been favorably exposed under a creative and enthusiastic teacher, he is likely to agree that it is great fun!

In addition, folk dancing is well-suited to coeducational and corecreational group. For teen-agers and young adults, it provides an easy way to achieve the needed sense of assurance and well-being that is necessary for good adjustment in mixed social group activities. Boys and men who would hesitate to take part in modern dance or ballet usually have no reservations about folk dancing. It can be carried on in very large classes almost as easily as in small groups. No special kind of costume is required, and the only equipment needed is a phonograph and a good collection of records. Finally, unlike many sports and games, folk dancing does not stress competition or require violent physical contact; injuries are therefore rare.

In summary then, the following might be listed as major folk dance values:

1. To develop desirable social attitudes through participation in a group activity.

2. To develop an understanding and respect for one's own national or ethnic heritage, and for that of other people.

3. To promote the most efficient use of the body, including coordination, speed, agility, balance, endurance, and grace, through the practice of fundamental motor skills and combinations of these skills.

4. To develop an appreciation of and interest in folk dancing as a leisure time activity, that may carry over into the years of adulthood.

5. To have fun.

For all these reasons, folk dancing has become more and more widely accepted in American education. From eighty to ninety percent of the schools and colleges investigated in recent surveys have reported that they offer folk dance instruction as part of their physical education programs.

### Folk Dancing in Recreation

Particularly during the past twenty years, there has been a similar widespread growth of interest in folk dancing as a recreational activity in community life. Among Boy and Girl Scouts, in groups for the handicapped or disturbed, in summer camps and adult resorts, in Youth Hostel groups, ethnic clubs and federations, in community centers, church and Grange halls, private homes, public parks and school gymnasia—more and more people have taken it up as an enjoyable pastime. Some dance in colorful ethnic costumes; others in their everyday clothes. Some belong to clubs, regional and state associations; others are unaffiliated. To some it has become a religion; others can take it or leave it. The pattern is as varied and vital as the topography of America.

A number of dance leaders and authorities have done much to stimulate this surge of interest in folk dancing throughout the United States. Outstanding among them have been Michael and Mary Ann Herman, who direct Folk Dance House and the Folk Dancer Record Company in New York City. These tireless leaders have made hundreds of excellent records and albums, trained other teachers, conducted summer camps and year-round workshops for over two decades. Vyts Beliajus, another inspiring figure in the folk dance field, has struggled against recurring illness to lead many folk dance institutes and popular dance groups, carry out extensive dance research, and publish a magazine, "Viltis," which has been an important source of information and critical thinking. On the West Coast, particularly in California where the movement has been exceptionally active, well-known dance leaders have included "Buzz" Glass, Walter Grothe, Chang, Lucile Czarnowski, Madelynne Green, and Lawton Harris, who directs the popular Folk Dance Camp each summer at the College of the Pacific in Stockton.

Other leaders have included: May Gadd, director of the Country Dance Society of America, Professor Ralph Piper of the University of Minnesota, the Dunsings of Chicago and the Collettes of Georgia, Dick Crum, an expert in Balkan dances, formerly at Duquesne University, and many others. Thanks to the efforts of all these leaders, there has been a steady growth of participation in recreational folk dancing throughout the country, particularly in the larger cities and on the West Coast.

### Folk Dancing vs. Round Dancing

In a number of areas, a conflict has developed between folk dance enthusiasts and those who prefer the recently composed American round dances. Proponents of each form of dance have criticized the dances done by the others and claimed superiority for their own type. This is unfortunate, for each kind of dance has its own appealing qualities.

1. The *folk dances* tend to be more physically vigorous and based on a greater variety of steps and formations, although many of them are quite simple. They are especially suitable for people who have an interest in intercultural activities and the folk arts, and for single individuals who lack regular partners to dance with.

2. The *round dances* are physically quieter and employ a limited number of basic steps, although many of them have long and complicated "routines," or step sequences. They have the appeal of being set to familiar, popular music, and are often enjoyed by middle-aged or older couples who like ballroom dancing but have never been particularly skilled at it—and who therefore appreciate having the routines made up for them.

The important point is that, just as there are different kinds of recreational dance, there is a public ready to participate in each kind. While they are *not* particularly compatible in mood and style, and are not usually done together, folk and round dancing are sometimes successfully combined on single dance programs. But the real dance enthusiast usually prefers a heavy emphasis on *his* favorite kind of dancing, which is only reasonable.

In most present day square dance clubs, the couple dances done during the evening are *round dances*. In school and college physical education programs, *folk dancing* is the more widely-found activity.

### Authenticity and Change

A somewhat similar dispute has arisen between those who are champions of authenticity in folk dancing and those who feel that it is unimportant, or who frankly and openly change or invent dances. Obviously, since there often are different versions of the same dance (as performed in different regions or by different groups) the word "authentic" has only relative meaning. To use it to describe a dance may mean that the dance was once done in a given time and place in this way, and was so recorded for posterity. It may mean that, in the judgment of an expert, the dance is clearly typical in form and style of a given nationality, or that the version presented has been widely observed in the present day. It may also imply that this is the version taught by a respected national authority, or shown by an exhibition group with a good reputation for traditional performance. As a rule, Michael Herman points out, adherence to such authentic forms makes for better dancing, and certainly does not reduce the fun of the dance.

On the other hand, when a dance is assembled for exhibition purposes, it *may* be done with a sincere regard for retaining traditional steps and style. Many nationality groups do this and a number of our most popular folk dances were originated in this way. Further, to say that a folk dance is anonymous in origin means only that we have lost sight of its creator. Somewhere, at some point, it had to be made up, and it is only fair to point out that many of our folk dances of today were once dances deliberately put together for exhibition purposes—or were even ballroom dances of an earlier period!

The real dispute comes when a choreographer borrows indiscriminately from various national sources and creates a "patch-up" job, or when a teacher deliberately or carelessly makes major changes in a dance. Such contrivances or distortions do folk dancing a disservice.

This book does not purport to be a major research effort into little-known dances, or the final arbiter when conflicting versions exist of the same dance. It simply attempts to present the most widely accepted and workable version of a large number of popular and appealing folk dances. Some have been performed in schools and recreational dance groups for many years; others have been introduced fairly recently. Each dance presented (with the exception of the round dances, labeled as such) has undergone the folk process, has been taught in the way shown by reputable leaders, and is, in the author's judgment, soundly constructed and enjoyable.

With this understanding of the "what" and "why" of folk dancing, let us move into the area of teaching techniques. The next chapter presents the basic positions, formations, and fundamental steps that every leader should know.

# Fundamental Positions,
# Formations, and Skills

······························· 2

THE FOLK DANCE teacher should be familiar with a wide variety of dances of different nationalities and levels of difficulty, if he is to be most successful.

He must also be able to explain and demonstrate the position, formations, underlying skills, and basic steps that form the substance of folk dancing. While actual dancing is invaluable in building a rich repertoire, the prospective teacher or leader *can* get much help from written directions and teaching guides, both in learning dances and how to teach them.

This chapter and the two that follow analyze the most important elements of folk dance instruction, in clear and simple language, with illustrations and diagrams where needed. The teaching techniques that are suggested may be modified by each leader to suit his own needs and purposes, as a matter of personal preference. Since many of the terms in this field have never been standardized, the leader may also wish to substitute some descriptive words for those used here. *Whatever* terminology is used should be consistently and logically applied.

## Folk Dance Formations

The formations most commonly found in folk dancing are shown here, together with the terms used to describe direction on the dance floor.

### Directional Terms

CLOCKWISE: the direction in which a clock hand moves. When dancers face the center, join hands and circle to the left, they are traveling *clockwise*. (Diagram 1)

COUNTER-CLOCKWISE: the opposite of clockwise. If dancers who are facing the center circle to the right, they are moving *counter-clockwise*. This is the commoner direction for most couple dances, and is known as the *line of direction*, or *line of dance*. (Diagram 2)

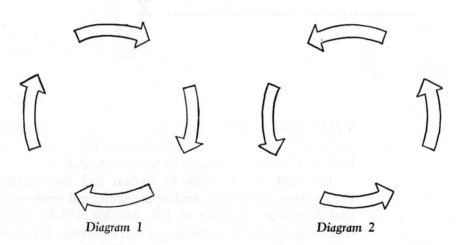

Diagram 1                    Diagram 2

### Formations

1. SINGLE CIRCLE, FACING IN. All dancers form a circle, facing the center of the dance floor, usually with hands joined. They may be with or without partners. (Diagram 3)

2. SINGLE CIRCLE, PARTNERS FACING. Couples form a single circle, with each girl on the right of her partner. Partners then face each other. (Diagram 4)

3. DOUBLE CIRCLE, COUPLES FACING COUNTER-CLOCKWISE. Couples stand side by side, usually with the girl on her partner's right; they face to the right (counter-clockwise). (Diagram 5)

4. DOUBLE CIRCLE, PARTNERS FACING. Usually the boy stands with his back to the center and the girl faces him. (Diagram 6)

Diagram 3

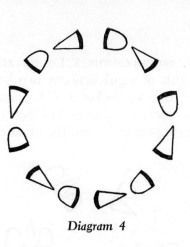

Diagram 4

Diagram 5

Diagram 6

Diagram 7

Diagram 8

5. DOUBLE CIRCLE, COUPLES FACING. Couples face each other in a double circle, one facing clockwise and the other counter-clockwise. (Diagram 7)

6. TWO COUPLE SETS, SCATTERED. Like the previous formation, but couples are scattered, rather than in a circle. (Diagram 8)

7. GROUPS OF THREE. Dancers stand in threes, usually with a boy between two girls or a girl between two boys. They may face the center or, more often, counter-clockwise. (Diagram 9)

8. THREES FACING THREES. Sets of three face each other in the circle, one set facing clockwise and the other counter-clockwise. (Diagram 10)

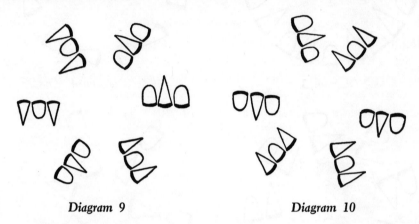

Diagram 9     Diagram 10

9. LONGWAYS FORMATION. A line of boys faces a line of girls, with the "head" or front end of each set near the source of music. (Diagram 11)

10. QUADRILLE OR SQUARE FORMATION. For four couples. One couple stands on each side of the square, facing in, with backs parallel to the walls of the room. (Diagram 12)

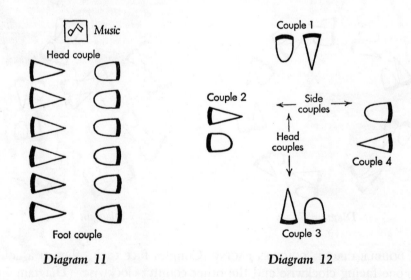

Diagram 11     Diagram 12

In addition to these ten, a number of other formations for teaching purposes or special dances are described elsewhere in this book.

Since the majority of folk dances are done by couples dancing by themselves or in sets with others, seven of the most frequently found couple dance positions are now described.

### Couple Dance Positions

1. CLOSED DANCE POSITION. Partners face each other, with shoulders parallel. Each person shifts slightly to his left, so he can look over his partner's right shoulder. They are somewhat farther apart than in the customary ballroom dance position; arms are higher and more extended. (Diagram 13)

2. SEMI-CLOSED POSITION. Partners keep the same hand position but turn to face forward, to the boy's left and the girl's right. His right and her left sides are adjacent. (Diagram 14)

(*above*)  Diagram 13

(*right*)  Diagram 14

3. OPEN POSITION. Partners stand side by side, with inside hands joined and free hands placed at waist. (Diagram 15) In some round dances, the

girl holds her skirt with her free hand, and the man places his free hand behind his back above the hip pocket.

4. SIDE POSITION. Partners stand in the closed position. If they shift to their own left, so right sides are adjacent, this is the BANJO POSITION. (Diagram 16) If they shift to the right, so left sides are adjacent, it is the SIDECAR POSITION.

(above)  *Diagram 15*

(left)  *Diagram 16*

(*left*)   *Diagram 17*

(*above*)   *Diagram 18*

5. PROMENADE POSITION. Partners stand side by side with the girl on her partner's right. Hands are joined (right to right, left to left) with the right arms above the left. (Diagram 17)

6. SHOULDER-WAIST POSITION. Partners face; each boy places his hands on his partner's waist, and she places hers on his shoulders. They lean slightly backward, keeping arms straight. (Diagram 18)

7. VARSOVIENNE POSITION. Partners stand side by side, facing forward. The boy is on the left and slightly behind his partner. He holds her left hand in his left, and her right in his right, slightly above shoulder level. (Diagram 19)

8. CONVERSATION POSITION. Partners stand side by side, facing forward. The boy's right arm is behind his partner's back, at waist level. Her left hand rests on his right shoulder. Free hands are usually as in Open Position. (Diagram 20)

In each position, the dancer strives to hold his partner firmly, but not so tightly as to constrict her movement. Each person supports his own

(left)  **Diagram 19**

(above)  **Diagram 20**

weight and, in closed position, there is often a definite "pulling apart" pressure. Usually, when hands are joined, the man's hand is turned so his palm is up, and the girl's hand is palm down in his.

Several terms used in describing dance position should be understood. These are:

INSIDE HAND OR FOOT: the hand or foot nearer the partner, when partners are side by side.

OUTSIDE HAND OR FOOT: the hand or foot farthest from the partner, when partners are side by side.

STARTING POSITION: when ready to begin a dance, each person usually has one foot free and slightly lifted, ready to move at the proper moment. This is known as the *free foot*. The foot bearing the body's weight is the *supporting foot*. The *free hand* is the one not in contact with one's partner at any moment.

## Underlying Skills in Folk Dancing

There are four stages involved in learning to folk dance, from a movement point of view. First, one must learn certain fundamental movements (which most people already know thoroughly). Then certain combinations of these movements, basic folk dance steps, and finally the folk dances themselves must be learned. To illustrate:

STEP 1. Two fundamental movements: the *step* (or walk) and the *hop*.

STEP 2. A movement combination: the *step-hop*.

STEP 3. A basic folk dance step: the *schottische*, based on the step and step-hop.

STEP 4. A popular folk dance: the Swiss *Meitschi Putz Di*, based on the schottische.

In this chapter, the first two stages of learning are analyzed. Chapter Three presents the basic folk dance steps, and the following chapters describe the dances themselves.

### Fundamental Movements

There are two types of movement skills we are concerned with: *locomotor* (traveling or "going somewhere" actions) and *axial* (movements performed in one spot on the floor, like stretching or swaying). Most of these are familiar to all of us, for we learned to do them as children. However, it is helpful to define and describe them exactly.

1. WALK. A familiar locomotor movement done in any direction and in an even rhythm (although it may be performed to varying meters and accents). The weight is transferred smoothly from one foot to the other, with one foot always in contact with the floor. As a foot takes the weight, it

does so first on the toe, then the ball, the sole, and the heel. At the exact moment of transferring weight from one foot to the other, both feet touch the floor.

2. RUN. A basic locomotor movement in any direction, in an even rhythm, to a faster tempo than the walk. At the moment of change from one foot to the other, both feet are briefly off the floor. The weight tends to be placed more on the ball of the foot than in the walk. The run is performed in various meters; when done in 3/4 time, it may be called a "running waltz."

3. LEAP. A spring off the floor in any direction, evenly transferring weight from one foot to the other, and with both feet off the floor. The leap may stress height, or distance, or be done in place. The knee bends slightly at the beginning and end of the leap, and the body's weight should be gradually absorbed by the foot and leg receiving it. Performed in a continuing series the leap resembles a slow run, but has greater "lift" off the floor.

4. JUMP. A spring off the floor (from one or both feet, and landing on both feet) done in any direction or in place. The toes are last to leave the floor and first to touch it in landing. The dancer absorbs the shock of landing by bending knees slightly and gradually taking the weight on the balls, the soles, and then the heels of his feet.

5. HOP. A spring from the floor on one foot, landing on the same foot again without a transfer of weight. In order to change the active foot in a series of hops, one must take another step between hops. Usually a hop has a duration of one beat; when combined with other steps, it may have equal time value (as in the schottische) or lesser value (as in the polka).

The *skip, slide, gallop,* and *step-hop* are all combinations of these fundamental movements, which are found in many folk dances.

6. SKIP. A walking step combined with a hop, which usually has one-half (sometimes one-third) the time value of the step. The skip therefore has an uneven rhythmic pattern. It is performed to 2/4 or 6/8 meter, two skips to a measure, with this accent: hop-STEP, hop-STEP. The skip is done in any direction and involves a transfer of weight, so the leading foot alternates: skip-LEFT, skip-RIGHT, skip-LEFT, skip-RIGHT. It is somewhat difficult to break the skip down into its parts when teaching it to children. However, since most of them know it already, the young child who does not can simply join hands with a partner who does and move around the floor with that person—gradually learning the rhythm and footwork.

7. SLIDE. A combination of two steps in any direction in an uneven rhythmic pattern (in 2/4 or 6/8 time, two slides to a measure). The first step is a gliding step with one foot, followed by a quick closing step with the other foot which takes the weight. This action of quickly displacing the supporting foot is called a "cut" step. In a series of slides, the same foot continues to lead: left-close, left-close, left-close, etc., *unless* the second action (the "cut" step) is

omitted, leaving the other foot free to start the next slide. The slide is usually done in a fairly rapid tempo, with the feet gliding smoothly, close to the floor. The slide, done slowly, may be called "step draw."

8. GALLOP. Similar to the slide, but done more vigorously, with knees lifted high, the gallop looks almost like a leap followed by a closing step. The same foot continues to lead, unless the closing step is not taken in the final gallop of a series—which releases the other foot to lead. As in the slide, the leap is given one half or one third the time value of the closing step.

9. STEP-HOP. A step in any direction or in place, followed by a hop with the same foot. This is in an even rhythm, with each action having the same time value. As in the skip, however, the leading foot alternates: (LEFT) step-hop, (RIGHT) step-hop, (LEFT) step-hop, (RIGHT) step-hop.

### Familiar Musical Terms

While an extensive knowledge of music theory is not necessary for the folk dance student or teacher, it is helpful to know some of the most important terms and concepts. A number of these follow:

*Time*, when related to dance music or rhythmic accompaniment, means a definite period of duration. The unit of measure for this is known as the *beat*; this is the underlying rhythmic pulse of a piece of music. *Accent* refers to the stress or emphasis which is placed on a beat or part of a beat. *Meter* describes the arrangement of rhythmic units (grouped into measures). *Tempo* describes the rate of speed of a piece of music, ranging from very slow to very fast.

To illustrate: melodies, when written out, are divided by vertical lines called bars into groupings of notes called measures. The time value and accent of the notes within each measure, and in a series of measures, create the musical rhythm. This is referred to as meter.

Several common meters found in folk dance music are:

2/4    This means that there are two beats to each measure, usually counted: *1* and, *2* and; *1* and, *2* and.

4/4    There are four beats to each measure, counted: *1, 2, 3, 4; 1, 2, 3, 4.*

3/4    There are three beats to each measure, counted: *1, 2, 3; 1, 2, 3.*

6/8    There are six beats in each measure, but only two of them, the first and fourth, are counted strongly. The effect is therefore very much like 2/4. This is counted: *1* and a, *2* and a; *1* and a, *2* and a.

If a dance is to be done accurately to the music, each step must be given a definite time value and fitted precisely to the meter. In most dances, a single movement of a part of the body is made to each musical beat. If two movements are made, the beat may be divided into two half-beats, and each movement carried out to one of these half beats. For instance, if four walking steps are done in a measure of 2/4 time (two beats to the measure) it would be done in this way:

| Count: | 1 | and | 2 | and |
|--------|---|-----|---|-----|
| Step: | 1 | 2 | 3 | 4 |

The next chapter includes an analysis of five basic folk dance steps, with suggested progressions for teaching them.

# Basic Folk Dance Steps

*THE MOST IMPORTANT* basic steps to be found in folk dancing today are the schottische, two-step, polka, waltz, and mazurka. Each of these had its roots in European folk dances done centuries ago, and each was part of the popular ballroom dance scene of the 19th century, here and abroad. Today, the waltz and to some extent the polka and two-step continue to be seen on ballroom dance floors in the United States. But it is as basic elements of folk dancing that they hold the greatest interest for us.

This chapter presents teaching guides for the schottische, two-step, polka, waltz, and mazurka. In each case, the procedure is to listen to the music, analyze and clap its rhythm, and then, slowly and carefully, learn the step pattern. This is usually done moving slowly in a forward direction, *without* partners. Only when the basic footwork has been learned do dancers take partners, learn to move in other directions, or turn as couples. Then they are ready to do a simple folk dance making use of the step they have learned.

### The Schottische

The schottische enjoyed its main vogue as a ballroom dance in America and Europe during the middle and latter part of the 19th century, but it is believed to have been a much older peasant dance, possibly of German origin. It is done as a separate dance, and also as part of many dances.

The essential action is this: three steps and a hop, usually performed in 4/4 time, with a movement on each count of the measure. When performed in this rhythm, the schottische is a smooth and even step. When done in 2/4 time, it becomes somewhat bouncier. Here is the exact step pattern:

1. Glide or step forward (or in any other direction) with the *left* foot, then the *right* foot, passing the left, and then *left* again. Hop on the *left* foot, keeping the weight on it, and freeing the *right* foot.

2. Repeat this action, leading with the *right* foot.

| Count: | 1 | 2 | 3 | 4 | 1 | 2 | 3 | 4 |
|---|---|---|---|---|---|---|---|---|
| Cue: | step | step | step | hop | step | step | step | hop |
| Footwork: | left | right | left | left | right | left | right | right |

Sometimes the second step simply closes to the first, rather than pass it.

In many traditional schottisches, particularly the old Military and Barn Dance schottisches, the two basic steps are followed by four step-hops. The action becomes:

Step-step-step-hop, Step-step-step-hop,
Step-hop, Step-hop, Step-hop, Step-hop.

The schottische may be done forward, sideward, backward, or with a turning action. In most European schottisches, the step is quite vigorous, with a lively hop. In typical American dances using the schottische, the action is more subdued, and the hop becomes a slight lift from the floor, with the free foot swinging forward, or lightly touching the floor.

#### Suggested Teaching Progression

1. Listen to a strongly accented schottische record in medium tempo. Clap the beat: four even counts, with the first beat of each measure accented.

2. In place, take three steps, lifting the free foot off the floor on the fourth count: Left-right-left-Lift RIGHT, Right-left-right-Lift LEFT.

3. Do this action moving counter-clockwise in a circle without partners or, preferably, in lines moving across the floor. (Diagram 21) Do this first to a clear verbal count, and then with musical accompaniment. Have the students make the lift of the free foot a *swing* forward. Have them *hop* on the supporting foot on the fourth count, as the free foot swings forward.

**Diagram 21**

4. Have them take partners and practice this action in promenade position, moving counter-clockwise. Always practice the action slowly first, have them do it with verbal cues and then to music.

5. Practice the basic schottische step in couples, moving backward and sideward. Gradually increase the tempo.

6. Add the familiar four step-hops at the end of the two schottische steps. Practice this going forward.

7. Have students practice going apart and together on the two schottische steps (leading with opposite feet) and then facing each other, taking shoulder-waist position, and doing the four step-hops turning once, clockwise.

8. Teach a simple dance making use of the schottische, like "Seven Steps."

## The Two-Step

The two-step was derived from the Gallopade, or Galop, a popular dance of the early 1800's believed by many to be of Hungarian origin, and became widely accepted as a ballroom dance toward the end of the 19th century. It was related to the foxtrot and is still done as one form of the foxtrot in Europe today. The two-step appears in many English and American round dances and is quite similar to the polka. In fact, it is a useful preliminary step in leading up to the polka.

The action of the two-step consists of three steps and a "hold," or "rest," to each measure of music played in 2/4 time. In detail:

1. Step forward with the *left* foot. Bring the *right* foot forward in a closing step, so the ball of the right foot is next to the heel of the left foot, and takes the weight. Step forward again with the *left* foot. Hold the weight on the left foot for one count.

2. Repeat the action, leading with the *right* foot.

| Count: | 1 | and | 2 | and | 1 | and | 2 | and |
|--------|---|-----|---|-----|---|-----|---|-----|
| Cue: | step | close | step | (hold) | step | close | step | (hold) |
| Footwork: | left | right | left | | right | left | right | |

NOTE: there is no additional movement during the "hold." The weight is simply held on the supporting foot. It sometimes helps to use other verbal cues, such as "Quick-quick-slow, quick-quick-slow," to get the idea of the rhythm across, or "LEFT-two-three, RIGHT-two-three," to emphasize the idea of leading with alternate feet.

### Suggested Teaching Progression

1. Have class listen to two-step music and clap the rhythm. First they may clap twice to each measure, on the accented beats: 1 and 2 and, 1 and 2 and. Then they may clap 1, 2, 3 (hold), 1, 2, 3 (hold), with *no* clap on the fourth count, to get across the idea of three steps in the "quick-quick-slow" rhythm.

2. In place, have them step to this rhythmic pattern: left-right-left, right-left-right.

3. Have them move across the floor (Diagram 21) doing the basic forward two-step, very slowly at first, then gradually speeding it up and adding musical accompaniment.

4. Have them join hands in a circle and practice the two-step to the left and then to the right. Have them move forward (to the center) four two-steps, and backward four two-steps. Repeat each progression until it is clearly learned and accurately performed by *most* of the class.

5. Have dancers take partners, and teach a folk dance like the "Jessie Polka," which uses the forward two-step in promenade or Varsovienne position.

6. To learn the couple turn, have the students practice first as individuals. All face one wall (East, for example). Each person steps to his *left* with his left foot, closes the *right* foot to the left, starting to turn to the left, and steps *left* again, continuing a left-face turn. At this point, he has completed the half-turn and is facing the West wall. Most of the turn has come on the *third* count. He again does a two-step, beginning with his *right* foot and doing a half-turn to the right, so he ends up facing the East Wall again. This is repeated, slowly at first, then faster, and with music, as dancers move across the floor toward the North wall, to this cue: "SIDE-close-turn, SIDE-close-turn."

7. This is now practiced by couples. They face, join inside hands and, starting with opposite feet, do the same action "face-to-face" and back-to-back" across the floor. (Diagram 22). The joined inside hands are swung forward and backward, to emphasize the half-turn.

**Diagram 22**

8. To learn the complete turn, in which couples move, or "spiral" across the floor, doing a clockwise (right-face) turn as a couple, have dancers release their partners' hands. Have them practice a right-face turn in place, simply taking four steps. Have them practice this moving across the floor, in order to get the feel of turning completely in the correct direction. Then teach the step: step with the *left* foot to the side, close with the *right* foot (starting to turn clockwise), and step diagonally backward and to the side with the *left* foot again, continuing the turn. This completes a half right-face turn. They repeat the action, beginning with the right foot, and continuing the turn: step *right* to the side, close *left*, starting to turn, and step *right* diagonally forward, completing the turn.

9. After they have practiced this individually, have them take partners. They do a closed, turning two-step, moving across the floor as in (8); the boy starting with his left foot and the girl with her right. It is helpful to keep the step short (particularly the girl on her first side-step) and to make the action smooth and continuous. On each two-step the couple turns halfway. They keep turning in the same clockwise direction and move across the floor in a continuous spiralling turn.

10. When most of the students have learned this, they practice the action in a double circle formation. As each couple rotates clockwise, it moves

counter-clockwise around the floor. Change partners frequently. At this point, introduce a dance making use of the turning two-step, such as the "Oxford Minuet."

### The Polka

The lively couple polka is said to have originated in Bohemia in the early part of the 19th century. It spread rapidly throughout Europe and America, becoming a dance craze first in Paris in 1844 and then in other world capitals. It has retained its popularity ever since, being done both as a free style dance, or as part of other dances. The style of the step varies from country to country: Lithuanian and Polish polka movement has a hop and springing little bounce throughout, while Czech and Russian polka dancers omit the hop and perform a step very similar to the two-step. The English polka has a crisp, lilting feeling, and the American step is robust and extended.

The polka is very much like the two-step. It consists of a two-step preceded by a quick little hop with a sixteenth-note value. The hop, which comes at the end of each two-step, thus serves as an upbeat for the succeeding step. The rhythm of the polka is uneven, with the second accented beat of each measure being held just a fraction longer, so the hop must be *squeezed* in before the next beginning beat. The effect is one of syncopation and the dance is quite bouncy. In detail:

| *Count:* | 1 | | and | 2 | and | 1 | and | 2 | and |
|---|---|---|---|---|---|---|---|---|---|
| *Cue:* | (hop) | step | close | step | hop | step | close | step | hop |
| *Footwork:* | (right) | left | right | left | (left) | right | left | right | (right) |

This is also very similar to the schottische, except that the hop, which takes a full beat in that dance, is very brief in the polka.

#### Suggested Teaching Progression

1. Students listen to polka music and clap in its rhythm, as in the two-step.

2. One simple approach to learning the step is to have students join hands in a circle and take four *sliding* steps to the left (*not* taking the weight on the right foot at the end of the fourth slide) and then four sliding steps to the right (not taking the weight on the left at the end of the last slide). Repeat this several times, first to a verbal count, and then with the music.

3. Have each person face to the right in the circle and practice the four slide steps forward leading with the left, and four slide steps leading with the right: LEFT-two-three-four, RIGHT-two-three-four.

4. Have them do the same action with two slides forward leading with the left foot, and two leading with the right. Gradually change the slide to a *gallop*, with knees lifted high, particularly on the first *slide* of each measure.

If the succeeding steps are kept quite short, this becomes a forward polka.

5. The teaching sequence suggested for the two-step may then be followed, using the *face-to-face* and *back-to-back* sequence (Diagram 22), and finally the couple turning action. The turn, as in the two-step, is a right-face half-turn on each measure.

### Alternative Method

If the students already know the two-step, have them practice it, making the steps short and bouncy, with a quick lift (growing into a hop) at the end of each measure, becoming part of the first step at the beginning of the next measure. This is done in a forward direction, and the teaching sequence describe above may then be used.

Because of its syncopated rhythm and catchy music, the polka is usually a lively, light and gay dance—especially enjoyed by teen-agers and young adults.

## The Waltz

The waltz is an extremely popular folk dance step, with a long and involved history. It apparently had its origin in 17th century Austria and was brought to England and France late in the following century. It has been a leading ballroom dance step and provides the basis of many round dances done today.

Essentially, the waltz is a combination of three smooth walking steps done to 3/4 time, with a complete transfer of weight on each step. The first two steps cover ground, and the third is a closing step. This may be described as *step-step-close*. One step is taken to each beat of the music, with alternate feet leading on the accented first beat of each measure. The balls of the feet are in light contact with the floor, and it is the smooth continuing turning step that gives the waltz its graceful appearance.

| *Count:* | 1 | 2 | 3 | 1 | 2 | 3 |
|---|---|---|---|---|---|---|
| *Cue:* | step | step | close | step | step | close |
| *Footwork:* | left | right | left | right | left | right |

The waltz takes several forms: the extremely fast, whirling Viennese step, the vigorous, stamping Bavarian Landler, the slower American ballroom waltz (sometimes called the Boston), and the moderately fast folk dance waltz, usually done with a half right-face turn on each measure.

### Suggested Teaching Progression

1. Play a slow, clearly accented waltz, and have the students clap: *1, 2, 3, 1, 2, 3*. Each note has an equal time value, but the first of each measure is stressed.

2. Students step in place, accenting the first beat with a slightly heavier step: *left*, right, left, *right*, left, right,

3. Moving across the floor, students take a *long* step on the first beat of each waltz measure, a *medium* step on the second, and a very *short* step on the third. Gradually, the third step is changed to a *closing* step. This is practiced first to verbal accompaniment, and then to waltz music. They may also practice the action moving backward, or traveling around the circle. It is important that the teacher emphasize that the second step is *not* a closing step. If done this way, the dance becomes confused with a two-step. While is it frequently done this way, it does not fit the music smoothly, and the action is jerky and awkward. The closing step *must* come on the third count of each measure.

4. As an intermediate step, before teaching the customary half-turn of the folk waltz, the teacher may teach a quarter-turn on each waltz measure. It is easiest to begin this with a box step in waltz rhythm:

| *Count:* | 1 | 2 | 3 |
|---|---|---|---|
| *Action:* | left (forward) | right (to side) | left (closes to right) |
| | 1 | 2 | 3 |
| | right (backward) | left (to side) | right (closes to left) |

After practicing this individually, each dancer takes a partner. They do the box step as a couple, the boy beginning forward with his left foot, and the girl backward with her right foot.

5. The box step is then converted to a left-face turn, by having the forward *left* step done with the toe turned *out* (making it a quarter-turn to the left), and the backward *right* step done with the toe turned *in* (continuing with another quarter-turn to the left).

6. Finally, the customary half right-face turn of the folk waltz is taught. Start by having couples join inside hands and move across the floor *face-to-face* and *back-to-back* (Diagram 22). To do this, each person does a half-turn away from his partner with the outside foot (boy's left, girl's right) on the first beat of the measure. On the second beat, he steps sideward in the line of direction, with the inside foot (boy's right, girl's left). On the third count, he does a closing step with the outside foot. At this point, partners are back-to-back, with the joined hands swung forward. The reverse is now done: each dancer takes a half-turn *toward* his partner with the free foot (1), reaches *sideward* in the line of direction with the outside foot (2) and again does a *closing* step (3). The dancers are now face-to-face again, in the beginning position.

| *Count:* | 1 | 2 | 3 |
|---|---|---|---|
| *Action:* | turn out | side step | closing step |

| Count: | 1 | 2 | 3 |
|---|---|---|---|
| Action: | turn out | side step | closing step |

Dancers practice this face-to-face and back-to-back action moving across the floor, and then moving as couples counter-clockwise around the circle. It is important to change partners frequently, whenever the instruction involves couples.

7. Finally, the continuous right-face turn is taught. Facing a side wall each dancer steps backwards on his left foot, toe turned in, and turning right (1). He steps to the side with his right in the line of direction (2). He closes left foot to the right (3) completing a half turn. He then steps forward with the right foot, toe turned out (1), sideward in the line of direction with the left (2), and closes the right foot to the left (3), completing the full turn.

8. After this action has been practiced individually, dancers take partners and practice it as couples. The boy begins by stepping backward with his left foot (toe turned in) as the girl steps forward with her right (toe turned out), and the turn continues from there. It is practiced across the floor, and moving counter-clockwise around the circle, with partners again being changed frequently. As they travel, dancers should avoid a zig-zag, jerky floor pattern. When moving across the floor, the line should be as straight as possible, and when going around the circle, gently curving.

Throughout, the step should be light and graceful, with the turn being done continuously. Steps should be fairly short, particularly the first step of each measure.

## The Mazurka

Like the waltz, the mazurka is done in 3/4 time. Originally believed to be a Polish folk dance, it became a popular ballroom dance in Europe and America during the last century. Today it survives as a step pattern found in a number of European folk dances and (in somewhat changed form) in the American "Varsovianna."

The folk dance mazurka involves a *step-step-hop* action. The dancer steps, or glides forward diagonally with the left foot (1), brings his right foot to the left with a closing step (2), and hops lightly on the right foot, lifting the left (3). As the left foot is lifted, the knee is bent and the foot swings back close to the right ankle.

| Count: | 1 | 2 | 3 | 1 | 2 | 3 |
|---|---|---|---|---|---|---|
| Cue: | step | close | hop | step | close | hop |
| Footwork: | left | right | right | left | right | right |

The same foot always leads in a series of mazurka steps, since there is no change of weight on the hop, *unless* some other action occurs to change the leading foot.

### Suggested Teaching Progression

1. Listen to mazurka music and clap its rhythm, marking an accent on the first beat of each measure, and a heavier accent on the second beat.

2. Step in place, left (1) and right (2) and hold the weight on the right foot on the third count. Practice this to verbal accompaniment first, and then to music.

3. Gradually lift the free left foot on the third count of each measure. Then add a hop on the supporting right foot as this is done.

4. Move forward, practicing this basic step with the left foot leading: left-right-hop, left-right-hop. Change the leading foot: right-left-hop, right-left-hop. Do this across the floor, and in a circle, moving counter-clockwise.

5. Leading with the left foot again, make the second step more of a "cut" step, coming in with a leap and sharply displacing the left foot. As the left foot is raised on the hop, it crosses slightly in front of the supporting right foot. The left foot is flexed and toe turned down. Practice the same action with the right foot leading.

6. Practice this basic step in couples and then introduce a dance using the mazurka, such as "Eide Ratas."

When the mazurka is done in European folk dances, it is danced with much spirit, the chest is high, the head turned in the direction of the movement, and the knee lifted sharply. In American dances, such as "Varsovianna," the hop is less pronounced or even eliminated, and the foot that would be lifted simply sweeps across in front of the supporting foot on the final beat of the preceding measure, to begin the action.

## Other Basic Folk Dance Actions

In addition to the five folk dance steps that have just been analyzed, there are many other actions which appear in folk and round dancing. Many of these are found in only one or two dances in this book; they are described when they occur. Others are used frequently enough to deserve being analyzed in this chapter.

BUZZ STEP. This step, the familiar "swing" of American square dancing, is also found in contra dances and a number of European folk dances, although the hand holds used may vary. Partners take a side position (Banjo), with their right sides adjacent, and right feet placed forward. The weight is on the forward foot. In rhythm, each dancer takes quick little pushing steps with his left foot, as he pivots in place on his right foot—which remains

forward. It is almost like a series of little slide steps, with the right foot leading, and the left foot kept behind the right.

CHUG STEP. This is a little like the "cut" step, except that the weight does
not come onto the displacing foot. With his weight on both feet, the dancer
moves to his left, pushing with the toe of his right foot, and almost "falling"
to his left side. This is usually repeated quickly several times, and is almost
like a buzz swing done to the side. It may be done in either direction.

CLOSING STEP. This action is frequently referred to in the description of
other steps. The free foot is brought up to the supporting foot, and takes the
body weight. If the foot is brought up, but does not take the weight, it is
simply a closed position, not a closing step.

CUT STEP. As described earlier, this is a quick displacement of one foot by
the other, done in any direction. If one stands on the left foot and brings the
right foot forward with a leaping action, putting the weight on it and displacing the left foot, that is a cut step.

GAVOTTE STEP. This old-time action involves three walking steps forward,
followed by a light touch of the free foot to the floor. No weight is taken on
this foot, which then becomes the leading foot.

GRAPEVINE STEP. Found both in American round dances and the folk
dances of other nations (particularly Israel), this is a series of side steps in
which one foot crosses alternately in front of, and behind, the other foot.
Thus: step left to side (1), cross right foot in front of left (2), step left to
side (3), cross right foot behind left (4).

PAS DE BAS. This is a modification of an old ballet action, the "pas de
basque." The dancer takes a step or spring diagonally forward and to the side
with his left foot (1). This is followed by a quick step on the ball of the right
foot in front of the left (2). Weight is held for a brief moment on the right
foot, and then the dancer steps backward in place on his left (3). Actually,
this may be done in either direction, and is usually repeated to the other side.

A somewhat less difficult version of the pas de bas: the dancer steps with
his left foot to the left, briefly touches the right toe across in front of the left
and lets it take the weight, before stepping with his left foot in place.

PIVOT. This is used to describe a partial or complete change of direction,
by an individual or couple. If an individual does it, he usually has his weight
on the ball of his foot and, without changing weight, simply turns smoothly.
Momentum forward or to the side is helpful in doing this. A "couple pivot"
is done by partners in closed position. Usually they make a full turn in a
specified number of steps, with a change of weight on each step. To pivot
smoothly, it helps if they are fairly close to each other (each person's right
foot forward between his partner's feet) but leaning slightly backward to
add to the force of the movement.

STAMP. This is a step which hits the floor heavily, but is quickly lifted so the stamping foot does not take the weight.

STEP-DRAW. A slow slide step, usually done to the side, in which the second (closing) step takes the weight.

STEP-HOP. As described earlier, this is a step and hop on the same foot, in an even rhythm (each action having the same time value). In a series of step-hops, the leading foot alternates: LEFT-hop, RIGHT-hop, LEFT-hop, RIGHT-hop.

STEP-SWING. The dancer steps on one foot, and swings the free foot from the hip in any direction (usually forward or to the side, in *front* of the supporting foot). In many folk dances, the action is done as a step-hop, in which the free foot swings lightly across in front, as the supporting foot *hops*. In some American dances, the supporting foot rises slightly on the ball, while the other foot grazes the floor as it swings across. This may be called a brush step.

WALTZ BALANCE. A frequently found action in the waltz. This may be done in one of two ways.

1. The dancer may step forward (or in any other direction) on the first count, and then bring the free foot forward, lightly touching it to the floor or against the ball of the supporting foot—but not letting it take the weight. Counts two and three are held in this position. The free foot is usually used to begin a balance step in the reverse direction. Thus there is just one change of weight in each measure.

2. In the second waltz balance, there are additional changes of weight. The dancer steps forward with the left foot, closes with the right foot, taking the weight, and steps with the left in place. The action is repeated in the reverse direction.

## Using These Basic Steps

As the next chapter makes clear, it is not necessary for an individual or a class to learn *all* of these basic steps and movements before beginning to folk dance. If too much time is spent in drill—the experience is likely to be boring and lifeless. Instead, real folk dances should be done as soon as possible. While enjoying these, the dancer will improve his execution of the basic steps. The teacher, of course, is alert to each student's progress and constantly helps him improve his understanding of the step and the style in which he performs it.

The next chapter describes the task of teaching the dances themselves, and offers many helpful guides.

# Folk Dance Teaching Guides

................................................ *4*

*NOW THAT THE* formations, couple positions, and basic steps of folk dancing have been analyzed, it is time to consider some of the problems of organizing and teaching a folk dance class. The following guides apply broadly to various kinds of groups, although each leader may wish to make special adaptations of the techniques described here in his own situation.

### Preliminary Arrangements

In most schools and colleges, folk dancing is taught in a gymnasium as part of the regular physical education program. Special facilities need not therefore be obtained. When a meeting place is chosen for a community folk dance group, the location must be accessible and the meeting time made convenient for those who are to attend.

It is best to allow approximately 15 to 20 square feet of floor space per student. A gymnasium that is 40 × 60 feet might thus accommodate between 120 and 160 students. Actually, the maximum number of participants for satisfactory teaching is somewhere around 60 (fewer than that, if they are children). Beyond this number, some students will be unable to see and hear the instructor properly and will lose interest and enthusiasm as a result. A smooth wood floor surface is best, but care must be taken not to wax it excessively. Surfaces like polished concrete, asphalt tile, black-top, and even grass are often danced on.

When phonograph records are being used for accompaniment, a suitable record-player and amplifier combination should be used. This should be portable, sturdy, and with a three-speed motor (with a fast-to-slow adjustment for each speed). Several companies, including Newcomb, Califone, and Bogen, make combinations specially designed for this purpose.

Most gymnasiums that have been recently built provide good acoustics, whereas in many older buildings the nature of the structure or the use of bare brick or plaster walls and ceilings creates echoes and sound distortion. The placement of the speakers at a good distance from the amplifier and the hanging of canvas or burlap sheets on the walls help to reduce such distortion and make it easier for the class to hear the teacher.

### Knowing the Group

The folk dance teacher should certainly consider the special characteristics of his students, including their physical vigor and well-being, their age, their national origins (if these are in any way unique), and their previous recreational and dance experiences.

He might ask himself, especially with regard to adult groups:

"Why have these people joined a folk dance class? To relax, find new friends, for exercise, or just out of curiosity?" "What is their age range—and what proportion of men to women?" "What special problems might they present?" Even when folk dancing is a *required* part of the program in school or college, the teacher should know the answers to these questions, to make the class as enjoyable as possible, and help the participants satisfy their personal needs.

### Developing Lesson Plans

Based on what he knows of the participants, the teacher then develops preliminary lesson plans.

The dances chosen would probably fall into a wide range, in terms of partner relationships, dance skills needed, nationalities represented, formation, level of difficulty, and physical effort required.

At the outset, the teacher should suit his material and teaching approach to the students with the lowest present level of ability—those who have had little experience in folk dancing. His purpose is to make every effort to help them learn the fundamental steps and experience success in their efforts. After a few class meetings, when these individuals have been given a chance to catch up, the teacher should aim at the class's general level of ability— possibly the middle seventy per cent or eighty per cent of the class. This means that he is trying to work effectively with the large majority. He does *not* ignore the poorest or best dancers, however. Through partner-changing, giving personal help, or using the more skilled dancers for demonstration purposes, he tries to satisfy the needs of each of these groups.

In any single class session, the teacher must: (1.) review previously taught dances, and (2.) add new dances or skills.

It is usually best to begin by doing familiar dances which are not too physically demanding, in order to *warm up* the group mentally and physically. In an adult recreation group where everyone may not arrive exactly at the starting time, this means that instruction of new dances is delayed until all are present.

Dances or skills which are new and require much concentration and effort should be taught in the middle of the class period.

The session should "taper off," ending with familiar dances that leave the students with a feeling of accomplishment.

Throughout, the teacher must strive for *balance*. Easy dances are alternated with difficult ones, strenuous with relaxing ones, and those being taught for the first time with "review" dances. A liberal number of "fun" dances or mixers are scattered through each class session, to provide for a gay, social atmosphere. If there are more of one sex than another, many circle dances that do not require partners, or "threesomes," are used.

Just like a home-builder, the folk dance teacher builds a foundation and then adds to it. As he progresses from simple to complex, he bases his instruction on previously learned skills. It is wise not to attempt to teach all the basic steps too quickly, but rather to start with dances that emphasize the fundamental movements. Then *one* folk dance step, such as the schottische, may be introduced. At this point, several dances using the schottische may be taught in a single session, thus firmly implanting knowledge of the step. In following class meetings, these would be reviewed, and gradually each new basic step would be introduced.

Throughout the process, the teacher also tries to improve the dancing style of members of the class. In general, most teachers find that it is better to do a lesser number of dances *well*, than to perform a great number in a sloppy fashion.

A number of carefully designed lesson plans for specific age levels may be found in Chapter Five.

### Teacher-Preparation

When a teacher is going to present a new dance or one that he has not taught recently, he should prepare himself carefully. First, he might listen to the music attentively, familiarizing himself with its tempo, spirit, and meter, as well as its various sections or parts. As he does this, he may scan the directions, to see how the actions fit the music.

Next, he should practice doing the dance, either by himself, or with a partner or group of dancers assisting him. This should first be done *without* music, working slowly from the directions, and then *with* music. If he understands the dance thoroughly the teacher is then ready to present it to his class. If any part seems unclear or does not fit the music smoothly, he must continue to work on it and, if necessary, get help from other experienced teachers or dance leaders. Finally, the teacher should make sure that he is familiar with the national style of the dance so that he can present it fully and authentically.

It is wise not to attempt to learn too many new dances all at once, but rather to build a repertoire gradually—dance by dance.

### Teaching A Single Dance

1. The first step in teaching any given dance is to have students take the required formation. If they have difficulty in choosing partners, suggestions may be found on page 39. For most groups, this would not be a problem.

2. The teacher may then play enough of the music to let the students know its spirit and tempo. He may also tell them something of the background of the dance—such as a colorful folklore anecdote or historical incident, which will make it more meaningful to them. This should *not* be a long-winded discourse.

3. To demonstrate the dance action, the teacher stands where he may best be seen and heard by all the dancers. In a circle, this would mean close to one side, facing across the circle. (Diagram 23) If the dancers are in lines,

*Diagram 23*

all facing one way (the best formation to teach certain steps), the leader may stand in front of them, or in their center, in a sort of "hollow square." He may also use a platform, although this is not desirable because it limits his movement too much.

The teacher breaks down the dance into sections (based on sequences of action that hold together as units) and slowly demonstrates the first section. The class then does this action slowly and carefully, as he gives "walk-through" instructions. This is done *without* musical accompaniment. If necessary, the boys' and girls' parts may be shown separately, and then combined.

The teacher then has the class do the action again, in a faster tempo, with rhythmic verbal commands and with music—if they are ready for it.

Succeeding sections of the dance are taught in this way, one at a time, and practiced by the class. As he continues to teach, the leader should move about from spot to spot, so no group of dancers is distant from him for very long, and all have a chance to observe the action from different angles.

When each part has been shown, the class reviews the entire action slowly, without music. The teacher may then perform it again with a partner, and without stopping, so they may see how it looks in its entirety. Finally, the class does the entire dance with musical accompaniment.

4. As the class does the dance, the teacher observes them carefully, and calls out verbal cues to help them anticipate each succeeding action. If the majority of dancers are getting the dance fairly well, he has them continue with it. If a sizable number are having difficulty, he should stop the dance, re-teach the sections or steps that are causing the most trouble, and have them try it again. If they should still have trouble, the teacher should analyze the possible reasons for this: his teaching method, level of difficulty of the dance, problems of acoustics or crowding, or the attitude and effort shown by the class. The experienced teacher learns to judge the ability of his class and rarely finds himself in a position where he must repeatedly stop a dance to teach it for those who are having trouble.

The leader should *not* over-teach, and must realize that as the dance progresses, many students clear up their own mistakes by watching others in the group, or being helped by their partners.

Several other general comments on teaching follow:

*Enthusiasm.* The teacher should be alive, dynamic, and enthusiastic; if he is, his students will probably mirror his spirit.

*Encouragement.* The teacher's approach should be optimistic and positive. Praise and encouragement do more than sarcasm and criticism.

*When Mistakes Happen.* When the teacher makes a mistake, he should neither ignore it nor try to "cover it up." The class will respect him for promptly correcting himself and teaching the dance properly. However, the teacher should be as well-prepared as possible; students lose confidence in a teacher who is always backtracking and contradicting himself.

*Student Alertness.* The need should be stressed for students to be aware of the music and its parts, to maintain proper dance position, to keep properly spaced out in the various formations, and to think ahead so succeeding dance transitions do not take them by surprise.

*Action Cues.* Students must learn to understand and respond promptly to such beginning signals as "Ready, and—" or "With the music, begin—." Other verbal cues, which are given during the dance to help the participants, should gradually be lessened as the dance is practiced so the dancers do not continue to rely on them, but develop their own memory of the action.

*Modifying Dances.* When working with children or beginners, the teacher may choose to temporarily modify certain steps or actions so they can be more easily learned. Thus, a forward two-step may be substituted for a turning couple two-step, or a walking step or skip may replace a step-hop. This is just a stage of teaching, however, and as soon as possible the correct action should be taught. It is important, wherever possible, to choose dances that may be taught in their entirety, *without* modification.

## Dance Styling

It is important to stress good dance styling at all times, so that moving gracefully and smoothly becomes a habit. Dancing is more than just moving aimlessly to music; it suggests dynamic, expressive, integrated movement of the body and all its parts.

*Posture.* The dancer should be erect, with his stomach in, chest high, head up, weight evenly distributed on the balls of both feet, and body inclined very slightly forward. The pose should neither be over-military or hunched over! Hand-grips are light but firm, and the free arms are held at the side in an easy, graceful curve, or with the free hands placed at the dancer's waist.

*Movement.* While step patterns are important in folk dancing, one should think of body movement as a unified action, of which the action of the feet is just a part. Thus, when the teacher says, "Step forward with the left foot," it is not a matter of the left foot going forward and the rest of the body somehow rushing to catch up. Rather, this idea should be conveyed: "The body moves forward, over the advancing left foot."

To maintain good balance and ease of movement, most dance steps should be kept short and light. When one foot passes the other, it usually moves very close to it. In most American dances, the feet travel close to the floor with a gliding effect. European folk dances have more hopping and leaping actions; in these the feet remain *under* the body for the most part, and the legs act with bending, spring-like movements that give strength and smoothness as the dancer leaves the floor and returns to it.

*Avoid Exaggeration.* The dancer should avoid excessive movements, such as twisting or bending the trunk too much, or bobbing up and down erratically. These are clumsy and unnecessary.

## The Group Climate in Folk Dancing

The achievement of desirable social outcomes for each student is an important objective of folk dancing. For this reason, and also because it is easiest to teach when a courteous, cooperative group climate prevails, the teacher must be aware of the social process in his class. It has already been stressed that his manner must be positive, encouraging, and friendly. Some additional suggestions follow.

*Partner-Taking.* The teacher may assist shy teen-agers or groups of single adults who are reluctant to take partners, in these ways:

1. He has them form two circles, one of girls and the other of boys. These circles rotate and, as they come together, individuals meet, pair off, and move in couples toward the front of the hall and around the side.

2. A similar approach is to have two lines formed, one of boys and the other of girls. They march forward, separate, go around the sides of the room and, as they come together again, take partners and come up the center (Diagram 24).

*Diagram 24*

3. Another teaching method which eases partner-taking is to form lines of boys, alternating with lines of girls, all facing the same gymnasium wall. After instruction has been given, the teacher asks the boys to face the line of girls and take the girl directly opposite them as their partner.

4. A final method is to begin by doing a dance in a large circle with no partners needed. When they have done this, each boy is asked to stand between two girls, which alternates them automatically. After they have shifted positions (and, since they are already out on the floor in a circle, they are likely to cooperate) each boy is asked to lift the hand of the girl on his right. She becomes his partner.

Each of these methods helps youngsters or beginning dancers take partners without actually having to go up to them and invite them to dance. They should then be ready to pick their own partners, in the next session.

*Formation-Taking.* At the outset, the teacher may help the dancers take formations (in dances with separate sets) by having one demonstration set formed and then by going around and counting couples or dancers off in the correct numbers, to form sets. Before long, dancers should be able to do this independently without the teacher's help.

*Partner-Changing.* In any group or class where there are mixed levels of ability, the more highly skilled dancers are likely to seek each other out as partners, since they enjoy dancing with each other. Thus the least capable dancers are left to pair off, and two groups are created, which are likely to progress at an unequal rate. One may be bored because the instruction is too slow for them; the other may be frustrated because it is too fast. To avoid this, the teacher regularly has each dancer take a new partner, either by using mixers, or by saying, "Each boy please move forward to the next girl. Take her as your partner for the next dance."

*Courtesy.* Students should be encouraged to have consideration for each other's feelings at all times. It is customary for the boy to approach the girl and ask her to dance; she is expected to accept, and each dancer thanks the other, when the dance is over. A dancer should never leave one set to join another until the sequence of dances he has been doing is ended. Students may help each other in a constructive way, but should never do so forcefully or belligerently.

At all times, each dancer should conform to the general floor pattern of movement, should be quiet during instruction, and should avoid behaving exhibitionistically.

*Disciplined Behavior.* The problem of discipline would rarely appear among adults, but may very well, among teen-agers. Since folk dancing is a coeducational activity that calls for much lively movement and some body contact, it may provoke boisterous behavior, laughter, teasing, and similar actions. Sometimes this represents an understandable teen-age reaction to confusion, or an attempt to cover up embarrassment, when a mistake is made. When this is the case the teacher may ignore it, or at most comment that it is helpful for the group to be quiet and attentive during instruction.

When a more deliberate disturbance is created—either vocal or physical— the teacher can usually control it by going over and speaking quietly to the individual or group that is responsible. Sometimes it may help to change a few students from one group to another; if necessary, those disturbing the class may be asked to sit down at the side of the gymnasium.

In the rare situation where an entire class may be misbehaving, the teacher may have them all sit down, point out the way they have been conducting themselves, and have them discuss the matter. Often the more responsible and mature students will make suggestions that will help control be established in the group. If this fails to work, it is likely that discipline is a matter that goes beyond the folk dance class and is a school-wide problem that needs to be dealt with on this level.

As a rule, if the dances are wisely selected and well-taught, and if the teacher's personality is warm and friendly, there will be *few* such behavior problems.

*Personal Appearance and Cleanliness.* A final aspect of folk dancing is that it *is* a social activity. As such, it provides an incentive to make oneself as attractive as possible. Each person should be neatly dressed in freshly laundered clothing that is suitable for informal dancing—not too heavy or constricting, and certainly not provocative in any way. Since students are likely to perspire during the more vigorous dances, the teacher should urge that they avoid offending their partners, through the liberal use of soap, water, and deodorants. It also helps, in this respect, if the gymnasium is kept fairly cool, which should be the case in any event.

# Planning Folk Dance Instruction Units

.................................................... 5

*IN CHAPTER FOUR* a number of useful guides are suggested for developing folk dance lesson plans. These deal with the selection of dances suited to the ability of the participants, and with maintaining good variety and balance in the dances presented in any single class session.

At this point, it is appropriate to suggest guides for planning extended instruction units for several different kinds of classes or groups. These include: 1. *elementary school* (grades 1—3); 2. *elementary school* (grades 4—6); 3. *junior and senior high school*; 4. *college classes* and *adult recreational dance groups*; 5. *Golden Age* and other special groups.

In each instance, six sample lessons—making use of dances found in this book—are presented. While they are only suggestive, and many other appropriate units might be devised for each group, they *do* demonstrate the approximate number of dances that may be presented within a given period of time, and the approximate level of difficulty for each group. They also show how, over a period of time, each dance continues to be reviewed regularly while new dances, involving a skill progression, are presented as well.

## Elementary School (Grades 1—3)

Children in any grade vary greatly, of course, in terms of their physical maturity, mastery of movement skills, and social behavior. In addition, there is obviously a great difference between first and third grade children. Nonetheless, certain characteristics of the entire age span may be noted. Children in these first three years of elementary school greatly enjoy rhythmic physical activity. Most of them can perform the basic locomotor actions of walking, running, skipping, sliding, jumping, and hopping. They can comprehend simple formations and partner-changing situations, and they enjoy singing games and pantomimic dances.

On the other hand, their attention span is limited and they often find it difficult to listen attentively to instruction. They are more "I" minded than group minded. In terms of motor skills, they are not yet ready to learn the basic folk dance steps such as waltz, polka, or schottische. The lesson plans suggested here take these factors into account. Most of the dances are suitable for the entire age range. A few may be a little too difficult for first-graders, but if they are modified (skip substituted for step-hop, or bow for balance) and played slowly these youngsters should be able to master them.

The time allotted per session is forty minutes.

*First Class Session*

Teach:   1. Kinderpolka, 2. Shoemaker's Dance, 3. Danish Dance of Greeting, 4. La Raspa.

*Second Class Session*

Review: 1. Kinderpolka, 2. Shoemaker's Dance, 3. La Raspa.
Teach:   4. The Wheat, 5. Carrousel.

*Third Class Session*

Review: 1. Carrousel, 2. Danish Dance of Greeting, 3. The Wheat.
Teach:   4. Chimes of Dunkirk (modified), 5. Rig A Jig Jig.

*Fourth Class Session*

Review: 1. Kinderpolka, 2. La Raspa, 3. Rig A Jig Jig.
Teach:   4. Bleking (modified).

*Fifth Class Session*

Review: 1. Carrousel, 2. The Wheat, 3. Chimes of Dunkirk, 4. Shoemaker's Dance, 5. Kinderpolka.

*Teach:* 6. Come Let Us Be Joyful.

**Sixth Class Session**
*Review:* 1. Chimes of Dunkirk, 2. Bleking, 3. Come Let Us Be Joyful,
4. La Raspa. 5. Rig A Jig Jig.
*Teach:* 6. Noriu Miego (slowly).

It is worth noting that the number of dances taught or reviewed in a single class grew from four, in the first session, to six, in the last. The reason for this is that children improve steadily in their ability to absorb instruction, to take needed formations, and to do a number of the actions which are common to all of these dances. In addition, once they have learned a given dance, it need not be taught again at length, but just reviewed briefly.

Some teachers may feel that too many dances are presented in each of these sessions, and that it would be more reasonable to teach only two or three, and to do these very carefully. The author is convinced that there is more than enough time to do each of these groups of dances within the forty-minute period, provided that over-drilling is avoided and that half the class time is not spent getting the children under control.

### Elementary School (Grades 4—6)

Children in this age range have much better physical coordination than their younger brothers and sisters in the lower elementary grades. Their strength, timing, balance, and rhythmic awareness are all improved. In addition, their attention span has lengthened and, while some of them may have become quite shy toward members of the opposite sex (and resistant to dancing with them as partners) their overall group behavior is much more responsible and cooperative.

All this makes it possible to teach children in the upper elementary grades a wide variety of new dances. In addition, several of those learned in the earlier grades may be continued, some of them in a more advanced form. It is wise to avoid too many couple dances at this stage, partly because of their attitude about dancing with members of the opposite sex, and partly because many of these dances involve folk dance steps in closed position—which these children are not quite ready to undertake. Some of the folk dance steps, such as the polka or schottische, may be introduced successfully in an open position, moving forward, however.

This is a forty-five minute class session.

**First Class Session**
*Review:* 1. Come Let Us Be Joyful, 2. Bleking, 3. Chimes of Dunkirk.
*Teach:* 4. Green Sleeves, 5. I See You.

**Second Class Session**

*Review:* 1. La Raspa, 2. I See You, 3. Green Sleeves.
*Teach:* 4. Circassian Circle, 5. Seven Jumps.

**Third Class Session**

*Review:* 1. Seven Jumps, 2. Bleking, 3. Chimes of Dunkirk, 4. Green
Sleeves.
*Teach:* 5. Alfelder, 6. Hora (simple version).

**Fourth Class Session**

*Review:* 1. I See You, 2. Alfelder, 3. Noriu Miego, 4. Circassian Circle,
5. Hora.
*Teach:* 6. Norwegian Mountain March.

**Fifth Class Session**

*Review:* 1. Come Let Us Be Joyful. 2. Norwegian Mountain March,
3. Seven Jumps, 4. Bleking, 5. Green Sleeves.
*Teach:* 6. Lot Ist Tod (with open polka), 7. Gustaf's Skoal.

**Sixth Class Session**

*Review:* 1. La Raspa, 2. Seven Jumps, 3. Lot Ist Tod, 4. Alfelder, 5. Hora,
6. Chimes of Dunkirk.
*Teach:* 7. Virginia Reel.

Here again the number of dances done in each class meeting increases
from five to seven during the six-meeting unit. This is partly because the
period of time itself is lengthened, and partly because the children themselves become more skilled and familiar with the dances they are doing.
The teacher should not try, however, to cram more and more dances into
each class session and should be willing to go more slowly occasionally, or,
when a dance involves a considerable amount of new instruction, as with
the Virginia Reel, to teach only one new dance at a session.

A number of dances in this group begin to teach the basic folk dance
steps. The second part of Bleking may be done with a forward step-hop at
the beginning, and during the fifth or sixth grades, may be changed to a
turning step-hop. Lot Ist Tod may be taught at first with a forward polka
step and then with a face-to-face, back-to-back polka, as preliminary to learning the actual polka in junior high school.

When a number of the couple dances become thoroughly familiar to
the children, they may be done without any instruction or review at all. After
announcing the name of the dance, the music is played immediately and
those few children who may not be sure of the step sequence can get their
cues from their classmates.

## Junior and Senior High School

Once again, there is a wide age spread here, and a tremendous difference between the mental and physical capabilities of the seventh and twelfth grader. Another factor is that the preadolescent or early adolescent is likely to feel shy and awkward and either to behave in an artificially restrained or overexuberant manner in a folk dance class. Partly because he wants so desperately to appear grown-up and to do dances that he considers sophisticated, the junior high school youngster may resist folk dancing, where the older student quickly recognizes it as good fun and takes part eagerly.

In spite of these differences, instruction in folk dancing through the junior and senior high school range should be thought of as a single, continuing progression. Therefore, they are dealt with together in this section.

Among the dances done in elementary school, which may be reviewed and continued, are the following: La Raspa, Bleking, Green Sleeves, Chimes of Dunkirk, Seven Jumps, Hora, Noriu Miego, Gustaf's Skoal, and Lot Ist Tod. The simpler, more childish dances would no longer be appreciated.

In junior high school the forward movements in waltz, schottische, polka, and two-step should certainly be taught, and each of these steps may also be gradually introduced in such dances as To Ting, Spinning Waltz, Masquerade, Doudlebska Polka, Seven Steps, and Road to the Isles. The mazurka is somewhat more difficult and may not be taught until somewhat later.

In addition to the couple dances, a wide variety of dances in formation should certainly be taught as well. These would include circle dances without partners, threesome dances, line and square dances, and many couple mixers, which are very useful in keeping a lively social atmosphere and assisting instructional goals.

The unit described here is geared for ninth or tenth grade, and for a fifty-minute class. Because there is more careful and drawn out instruction of actual steps, it is likely that fewer dances may be done in a given session than was true during the elementary grades.

### First Class Session
*Review:* 1. Hora, 2. Circassian Circle.
*Teach:* 3. Seljancica Kolo, 4. Road to the Isles, 5. Seven Steps.

### Second Class Session
*Review:* 1. La Raspa, 2. Seven Steps, 3. Road to the Isles.
*Teach:* 4. Ersko Kolo, 5. Jessie Polka.

### Third Class Session
*Review:* 1. Seljancica Kolo, 2. Road to the Isles, 3. Jessie Polka, 4. Lot Ist Tod (with couple turning polka).

*Teach:* 5. Kalvelis.

**Fourth Class Session**

*Review:* 1. Ersko Kolo, 2. Lot Ist Tod, 3. Seven Steps, 4. Kalvelis.
*Teach:* 5. Doudlebska Polka, 6. Puttjenter.

**Fifth Class Session**

*Review:* 1. Road to the Isles, 2. Doudlebska Polka, 3. Seljancica Kolo,
4. Jessie Polka.
*Teach:* 5. To Ting.

**Sixth Class Session**

*Review:* 1. Lot Ist Tod, 2. Seven Steps, 3. Ersko Kolo, 4. Jessie Polka,
5. Kalvelis, 6. To Ting.
*Teach:* 7. Masquerade.

In this instructional sequence, the schottische is taught first, in a cluster of related dances: Seljancica Kolo, Road to the Isles, and Seven Steps. The forward two-step and polka and the turning polka are next taught in Jessie Polka, Lot Ist Tod, Kalvelis and Doudlebska Polka and, at the same time, the schottische continues to be reviewed. If time permits, new schottische dances would be introduced. Finally, the open and closed waltz is learned in To Ting, and reviewed in Masquerade. In future classes, the mazurka would be taught and each of the basic steps would be experienced again and again in different couple and formation dances.

## College Age and Adult Folk Dance Groups

In planning instructional units for young adults in college physical education classes or community recreation groups, any of the folk dances found in this book—except those obviously for young children—are suitable. If the members of the class or group have had very little folk dance background, they might logically start with some of the dances recommended for junior high school which emphasize the teaching of basic skills. If they have already had a good background, they may wish to attempt some of the more advanced dances, such as Meitschi Putz Di, Neapolitan Tarantella, Windmueller, Kreuz Konig, or Black Nag. In either case, the teacher must be careful to plant necessary learnings in advance, so that when a difficult dance is tackled, most of its component parts, floor patterns, etc., have already been learned.

Even with a group that is capable of doing advanced dancing, it is wise to do a healthy number of easy, relaxed, and familiar dances interspersed among the others. Folk dancing should be *fun* and too much concentration on learning new material tends to lessen the enthusiasm of many participants!

Another factor to be considered is the physical vigor of the participants. College students and young adults (in their twenties or early thirties) are usually at their height of strength and energy, and are willing and able to consume a heavy diet of Balkan dances and other vigorous numbers. Those who are older, in community recreation groups, tend to be more easily tired and often prefer the quieter couple dances, or progressive circle or contra dances which are less strenuous.

Most college folk dance classes would probably be about fifty minutes or an hour in length, while adult folk dance clubs are likely to meet for two hour sessions or longer. As a compromise, the sample program described here is for a ninety-minute session. It is purely hypothetical, and for a group with "average" background.

### First Session

*Teach:* 1. Misirlu, 2. Road to the Isles, 3. Sellenger's Round, 4. Three Man Schottische, 5. Portland Fancy, 6. Boston Two-Step, 7. To Ting.

### Second Class Session

*Review:* 1. Boston Two-Step, 2. Three Man Schottische, 3. Portland Fancy, 4. To Ting, 5. Sellenger's Round.

*Teach:* 6. Nebesko Kolo, 7. Kalvelis, 8. Korobushka.

### Third Class Session

*Review:* 1. Korobushka, 2. Kalvelis, 3. Road to the Isles, 4. Nebesko Kolo, 5. Misirlu.

*Teach:* 6. Masquerade, 7. Dashing White Sergeant, 8. Fireman's Dance, 9. Kuma Echa.

### Fourth Class Session

*Review:* 1. Boston Two-Step, 2. Portland Fancy, 3. Kuma Echa, 4. Road to the Isles, 5. Dashing White Sergeant.

*Teach:* 6. Seven Steps, 7. Spinning Waltz, 8. Little Man in a Fix, 9. Ve' David.

### Fifth Class Session

*Review:* 1. Seven Steps, 2. Fireman's Dance, 3. Kalvelis, 4. Misirlu, 5. Sellenger's Round.

*Teach:* 6. The Rifleman, 7. Virginia Reel, 8. Meitschi Putz Di.

### Sixth Class Session

*Review:* 1. Nebesko Kolo, 2. Korobushka, 3. Spinning Waltz, 4. The

Rifleman, 5. Kuma Echa, 6. Meitschi Putz Di.
*Teach:* 7. Black Nag, 8. Haymaker's Jig.

The chief point of this simple unit outline is to show a variety of dances, most of them simple or intermediate in difficulty, that may be included in an instructional program. A second aspect is the way in which skill progressions are achieved. It is wise to do the Boston Two-Step, for instance, before Dashing White Sergeant, because it gives practice in the pas de bas. The Dashing White Sergeant because of the Reel of Three is helpful preparation for Black Nag, as is Sellenger's Round because of many of the steps it teaches. Portland Fancy leads to Fireman's Dance, and both are helpful in preparation for the contra dance, Haymaker's Jig.

While a teacher must not think exclusively of this kind of progression, it is helpful if he keeps it in mind, particularly when approaching the more difficult dances.

### Golden Age and Other Special Groups

There is an increasing use of folk dancing today with various kinds of special groups, such as Golden Age Clubs (Senior Citizens), mental patients, or similar groups, where the participants have specific limitations or handicaps. With each of these, the important thing is to make sure that you understand the people involved—their emotional and social needs, *and* their physical and mental limitations. Older people, for instance, often have a variety of handicaps: they have poor hearing and vision, their strength and endurance have been impaired, their motor coordinations and sense of balance may have been affected—and, of course, they are more brittle, so a fall may have serious consequences.

For this reason, only the simplest and slowest dances would normally be done with Golden Age groups. Dances such as the Varsouvianna, Glowworm Mixer, Oklahoma Mixer, or a number of the waltzes, when played slowly, are quite acceptable. Many of the easiest children's dances would work well with Senior Citizens, except they are recognizable as children's dances, and therefore might be distasteful to them. Some older people who have retained their vigor may be found dancing strenuous, difficult dances in company with younger adults, but by and large, the above restrictions are indicated for most Golden Age groups.

In mental hospitals, provided that the patients are in fairly good touch with reality and able therefore to respond to instructions, a wide variety of dances may be done. They may be fairly demanding physically, but should not be too complex in footwork or floor patterns. The author has had considerable success with mental patients using such dances as: Ersko Kolo,

Spinning Waltz, Chimes of Dunkirk, La Raspa, St. Bernard's Waltz, Teton Mountain Stomp, Oh, Susanna, All-American Promenade, Seven Steps, and a good selection of square dances as well.

## Other Guides for Instruction

*Keeping Records.* The leader of any folk dance class or group that meets regularly over a period of time should keep an accurate record of each session. While he may be wise to plan a series of classes in advance, he should also be flexible enough to change his plans, depending on the situation and the progress the class is making. A helpful record form would include:

| Dance Title | Country | Formation | Steps | When Used | When Taught | When Reviewed | Comments |
|---|---|---|---|---|---|---|---|

Keeping such a record, meeting by meeting, will help the leader maintain an accurate check on the progress of his class or group and the kinds of dances or skills they have been working on. For teachers who work with large numbers of students it is essential.

## Promoting Motivation and Interest in Folk Dancing

In school or college folk dance classes, it is advisable to plan assignments or additional projects to heighten interest in the activity. These may include:

1. Having students watch for and keep clippings of magazine articles and picture stories about folk, square and ethnic dancing. They may develop individual scrapbooks or class bulletin boards or displays.

2. Obtaining and showing films on folk dancing of different countries to the class. Some of these may be obtained from Dance Films, Inc., 130 W. 57 St., New York, N.Y.

3. Assigning readings and reports on the folk dance customs of other lands. Since, in class, there is usually little time for the teacher to lecture on these subjects (and his background is necessarily limited in many cases) students may be given suggestions for readings (see page 217). As part of such an assignment, groups of students may carry out detailed projects in which they explore the folk customs, stories, songs and costumes of a particular country, in connection with other classes in the language arts or social studies.

4. Having classes visit national groups that perform their traditional dances. Usually this is possible only in large cities or areas with ethnic groups (Scandinavian, Slav, etc.) that have remained somewhat distinct. While most of these are gradually losing their identities, some have made

a point of preserving their folk heritage with pride and care, and seeing them in action is an exciting experience for young students of folk dancing.

5. Organizing and promoting folk dance festivals. These provide an excellent means of stimulating interest and motivation, and are described in detail in the final chapter of this book.

### Evaluating Outcomes of Folk Dancing

The recreational dance leader in a community group does not usually think consciously about evaluating the outcomes of his teaching; it is usually enough for him to know that the participants are having fun, and that the level of attendance remains high. The school or college instructor, on the other hand, is expected to have specific goals and objectives in mind. He must make a deliberate effort to measure the outcomes of instruction, both to help him grade students on their progress and to determine how effective his own teaching has been.

Such goals usually fall into three categories:

1. *Knowledge.* The teacher tries to impart knowledge of fundamental folk dance movements, steps, and formations, and of a wide variety of dances and their origins, as well as general information about folk dancing and the allied folk arts, particularly music.

2. *Skills.* The student is expected to be able to dance smoothly in various rhythms, with a poised, well-coordinated body, performing each movement accurately, with carefully spaced out and graceful floor patterns, and appropriate style for each dance.

3. *Attitudes and Appreciations.* Each student should demonstrate pride in his own performance, satisfaction with the activity, and a cooperative attitude toward other group members. A heightened interest in folk lore and increased appreciation of those of other national origins are also desirable outcomes of folk dance participation.

How is all this to be measured?

1. KNOWLEDGE MAY BE TESTED IN THE FOLLOWING WAYS:

a. Short-answer paper-and-pencil tests provide an objective means of discovering a student's knowledge of dances, step combinations, or the background and history of folk dancing. Sample questions:
*Little Man in a Fix* is a: ———— circle dance without partners; ————
line dance; ———— two-couple dance (check correct answer).
The *schottische* is usually performed in 6/8 time.
   True or false?
Describe the action known as *ladies chain* in a sentence or two.

b. Students may be given a recognition test. The teacher plays a number of folk dance records, and students may be asked to identify each one with respect to: name of dance, nationality, formation, and steps employed.

c. If the class is small enough, the teacher may hold a discussion at the end of the folk dance unit, to discover how well students have understood and retained the material taught.

2. SKILLS CAN BEST BE MEASURED THROUGH DIRECT OBSERVATION IN A PERFORMING SITUATION. Ideally, if a class is small enough, the teacher would know each student and be able to observe him from session to session, noting his progress and improvement in performance. If this is not feasible, in a large class, the teacher may plan a testing period in which the students are asked to show their knowledge of a number of dances they have had—and with which they should be familiar. Each student has a large number pinned on his back, to help if his name is not known to the teacher. The teacher plays a number of records, and students perform the dances. He rates them, making quick notes against their names (keyed to numbers) on the class roster, with respect to the following points:

a. Knowledge of the steps and floor patterns.
b. Rhythmic ability.
c. Grace and proper style.
d. Body control and coordination.
e. Accuracy of floor pattern.

As he watches them, he may note specific strengths and weaknesses of each student, or may rate them according to a scale (5=excellent, 4=very good, 3=good, 2=fair, 1=poor) on each of the above points. Partners and groups would be rotated after each dance, so students would not be handicapped by having weak partners throughout. Over a full period of observation, a teacher should be able to make enough notations to make a reasonable judgment as to each student's skill.

3. ATTITUDES AND APPRECIATIONS. These are difficult to measure objectively and can best be observed over a period of time, with respect to the following points:

a. Each student's interest, effort and enthusiasm in the activity, as displayed during class.
b. Willingness to help each other; active participation in special events or folk dance projects (visitations, assembly programs, festival committees, etc.)

In addition to *his* rating the students, a teacher may also have *them* rate him. This can be done through the use of an anonymous rating form or check list, through which they may make comments or suggestions about his teaching methods and the entire organization of the class, as well as the dances that have been presented. Many suggestions (such as: "Your instruction is too fast," "I like everything about the class," "Don't make fun of those who can't do the dances," or "Why do we do the same boring dances day after day") may come from such an evaluation. Some may be justified and others not—but they will all be helpful to a teacher in letting him know how his students view the class.

# Easy Folk Dances for Elementary Grades

............................................... *6*

THIS CHAPTER PRESENTS twenty folk dances of varying levels of difficulty, which are most useful for children in the elementary grades. They may also be taught to beginning dancers in junior high or even secondary school, and some of them are excellent "fun dances" for adult folk dance groups.

A teacher might ask, "What makes a folk dance suitable for young children?"

1. The music should be simple and clear, with the rhythm and sections of melody clearly recognizable.

2. The action should be based on clapping, stamping, sliding, walking, and hopping, rather than on the more complicated folk dance steps described in the previous chapters. In general, the movement of the dance should be fairly full and vigorous, rather than precise, small, or subtle.

3. Each dance should have a limited number of parts; two or three are usually as many as young children can remember and perform accurately.

4. If possible, each dance should be connected in some way to a folk custom or heritage that will be interesting to children, or have some element of pantomimic action that makes it entertaining for them.

5. The formation and pattern of floor movement should be simple and partner-changing, when it occurs, should flow smoothly.

### The Dances in this Chapter

The twenty-one dances presented here are all traditional. Most of them were first presented and used in American physical education and recreation programs for children about forty or fifty years ago. They have been widely used since. None are new or unique or freshly discovered, but for the child of elementary school age, who is learning to folk dance for the first time, this is not important. The dances are *all* new to him, and the tried-and-true ones are likely to be the most successful.

Twelve different nationalities, predominately northern European, are represented. Included are simple couple dances, partner-changing dances, dances in a circle without partners, play party games (American singing mixers), two-couple dances, and dances for three.

Each dance has been broken down into action sequences and carefully described. For suggestions on how to use the descriptions, see the Preface and pages 36 to 41. To help the beginning teacher, each dance is assigned an approximate level (based on the growth characteristics of children) at which time it may be introduced. Since individual children vary (as do classes or schools) teachers should feel free to present dances a grade or two before or after the levels suggested here.

Suitable phonograph records are suggested for each dance. In some cases, these are over-long and the teacher may wish to lift the needle after several repetitions of the dance, rather than go through the entire record.

# Danish Dance of Greeting

•••••••••••••••••••••••••••••••••••••••• DENMARK GRADE ONE

A light and pleasant little dance, done in a spirit of friendly greeting.

*Formation:* Single circle of couples, facing center.

### Part One. (MUSIC A)

MEAS. 1—2. Each child claps his own hands twice and then bows (or curtseys) to his partner. He again claps his hands twice and bows or curtseys to his corner (neighbor on the other side).

MEAS. 3—4. Each child stamps twice in place, *RIGHT* and *LEFT*, while facing the center, and then turns around in place (turning away from his partner) in four quick steps.

MEAS. 5—8. The action of Meas. 1—4 is repeated.

### Part Two. (MUSIC B)

MEAS. 1—4. Children join hands and circle left with sixteen running steps.

MEAS. 5—8. They circle right with sixteen steps.

NOTE: Children may enjoy singing out, "Clap! Clap!—" and calling out the name of their partner (or corner) on the next count.

RECORD: Folkraft 1187.

# Shoemaker's Dance

•••••••••••••••••••••••••••••••••••••••• DENMARK GRADE ONE

In ancient days, skilled craftsmen who belonged to guilds in Europe often had their own occupational dances, to be done on special holidays. This dance is an example of these, and was brought to America in 1917, as done by the Danish Folk Dance Society. The words are:

A. *Wind, wind, wind the bobbin; wind, wind, wind the bobbin,*
   *Pull, pull, tap, tap, tap!*
   *Wind, wind, wind the bobbin; wind, wind, wind the bobbin,*
   *Pull, pull, tap, tap, tap!*

B. *Tra-la-la-la-la-la-la* (sing four times).

*Formation:* Double circle of couples with partners facing, boys with backs to center. Hands are placed on hips.

**Part One.** (MUSIC A)

MEAS. 1. With forearms held up in front of his chest, each child rapidly rotates his clenched fists forward, around each other, three times, "winding the thread."

MEAS. 2. This action is done in the reverse direction, backward.

MEAS. 3. Each child pulls his elbows apart and backward sharply, twice, "pulling" the thread to tighten it.

MEAS. 4. Each child strikes his clenched left fist smartly with his right fist, three times, "driving the pegs." At the same time, he taps his right foot forward, three times.

MEAS. 5—8. Action of Meas. 1—4 is repeated.

**Part Two.** (MUSIC B)

MEAS. 1—8. Partners join inside hands, with free hands on hips and skip forward (counter-clockwise) sixteen steps. This may later be taught as a forward polka step, as a lead-up to teaching the polka.

RECORD: RCA Victor LPM 1624, Folkraft 1187.

## The Wheat

•••••••••••••••••••••••••••••••••  CZECHOSLOVAKIA    GRADE TWO

This easy but enjoyable dance for three appeared originally in 1917 in a collection called "Folk Dances of Bohemia and Moravia," by Anna Spacek and Neva Boyd. Its action is similar to the German dance, "Come Let Us Be Joyful," which follows it.

*Formation:* Sets of three (one boy and two girls, or vice-versa), with inside hands joined, all facing counter-clockwise around the circle (Diagram 9).

**Part One.** (MUSIC A)

MEAS. 1—8. All walk heavily forward, sixteen steps.

**Part Two.** (MUSIC B)

MEAS. 1—8. The center child joins right elbows with the child on his right and they turn or swing twice around, with eight skipping steps. He does the same action with the child on his left, joining *left* elbows and skipping around eight steps.

NOTE: As a variation, each time the dance is repeated, the center child may move forward to the next group.

RECORD: RCA Victor LPM 1625.

# Carrousel

This dance suggests a merry-go-round which starts slowly and then speeds up. At the end, when partners change places, they are getting aboard for another ride. The words are:

A. *Little children, sweet and gay, carrousel is running.*
   *It will run till evening. Little ones a nickel,*
   *Big ones a dime. Hurry up, get on board,*
   *Or you'll surely be too late!*

B. *Ha, ha, ha, happy are we, Anderson and Peterson and Lundstrom and me!*
   *Ha, ha, ha, happy are we, Anderson and Peterson and Lundstrom and me!*

*Formation:* A double circle of couples facing the center. Girls, in front, have hands joined in a circle. Each boy stands *behind* his partner and places his hands on her shoulders (Diagram 25).

*Diagram 25*

### Part One. (MUSIC A)

MEAS. 1—8. Each child does sixteen slow sliding steps, or step-draws, to his own left (two steps per measure).

### Part Two. (MUSIC B)

MEAS. 1—8. As the music accelerates, each child does sixteen fast sliding steps, still to his left, in double time, with four slides per measure.

MEAS. 1—8. This fast sliding action is now done to the right, with sixteen fast steps. At the end, boys and girls immediately *change* places, so the boys are in front, with hands joined, and the girls behind with hands on their partners' shoulders. Each time the dance is repeated, this is done.

NOTE: The dance should be practiced slowly and carefully, particularly the second part, so that children expect the change of direction and are not "thrown off" when the merry-go-round reverses itself.

RECORDS: RCA Victor LPM 1625, Folkraft 1183, Educational Dance Recordings FD-1.

## ✓ *Kinderpolka*

•••••••••••••••••••••••••••••••••••••  GERMANY          GRADE TWO

In spite of its name, which means "children's polka," this simple little dance does not include a polka step. Children enjoy its "scolding" action.

*Formation*: Form a single circle of couples, with each girl on the right of her partner as they face the center (the girl is *always* on the right, unless otherwise specified). Partners face each other and join hands, with arms extended to the side at shoulder height.

### *Part One.* (MUSIC A)

MEAS. 1—2. Moving to boy's left and girl's right, couples take two step-draws toward the center (step-close, step-close) and then three light stamps in place.

MEAS. 3—4. They repeat this, *away* from the center, starting with the boy's right and the girl's left: step-close, step-close, stamp-stamp-stamp.

MEAS. 5—8. Action of Meas. 1—4 is repeated.

### *Part Two.* (MUSIC B)

MEAS. 1—4. Each child claps his own thighs once with both hands, claps his own hands together once, and claps both hands against his partner's hands three times. The count is: *knees* and *hands* and *one-two-three*. This entire action is repeated.

MEAS. 5—6. Each child lightly springs on the left foot in place, at the same time placing his right heel forward and shaking his right forefinger at his partner three times with a "scolding" motion. The action is repeated with the left heel and forefinger.

MEAS. 7—8. Each child turns to the right, in place, with four steps, faces his partner and stamps three times.

RECORDS: RCA Victor LPM 1625, Folkraft 1187, Educational Dance Recordings FD-1.

## I See You

Here is a slightly more difficult singing game, which children in the middle elementary grades will find interesting. The words are:

A. *I see you, I see you, Tra la la la la la.*
   *I see you, I see you, Tra la la la la la.*

B. *You see me and I see you, then you take me and I'll take you,*
   *You see me and I see you, then you take me and I'll take you.*

**Formation:** Sets of two couples facing each other, each girl, with hands on hips, standing in front of her partner, whose hands are on her shoulders. Several such sets may stand in a line (Diagram 26).

**Diagram 26**

**Part One.** (MUSIC A)

MEAS. 1—2. The boy in back leans to his left, bending from the waist, so he can "peek" at the opposite boy. He then leans to his right, and "peeks" again at the opposite boy.

MEAS. 3—4. He repeats this action twice as fast, to the left, right, left, and hold.

MEAS. 5—8. The action of Meas. 1—4 is repeated, starting to the right. The teacher may cue this entire part, by calling out, "Slow, Slow, quick-quick-slow, Slow, Slow, quick-quick-slow," *or,* "LEFT and RIGHT and one-two-three, and RIGHT and LEFT and one-two-three."

**Part Two.** (MUSIC B)

MEAS. 1—4. The boys clap their hands on the first count and skip past their partners' left sides with four steps. Each boy joins hands with the opposite boy and they turn with four skipping steps.

MEAS. 5—8. The boys clap again, return to their partners with four skips, join hands with them and turn with four skipping steps. They resume the beginning formation, with the boys *in front*, and the girls *behind them*. This time the girls perform the action from the beginning, first doing Part One and then skipping out to swing the opposite girl, in Part Two.

RECORDS: RCA Victor LPM 1625; Educational Dance Recordings FD-1.

## *Chimes of Dunkirk*

•••••••••••••••••••••••••••••••••••••••••  F R A N C E          GRADE THREE

This dance comes from the coastal region of France (close to Belgium) where the famous evacuation of World War II British troops took place. The music tells us of the age-old church chimes ringing out in the town of Dunkirk.

*Formation:* Couples form a double circle, boys with backs to center.

*Part One.* (MUSIC A)

MEAS. 1—2. All stamp three times, left-right-left (boys with arms crossed in front of chest, and girls with hands on hips). Hold on fourth count.

MEAS. 3—4. All clap hands three times. Hold on fourth count.

MEAS. 5—8. Joining hands with partners, each couple walks once around to the left (clockwise), returning to place in eight steps.

*Part Two.* (MUSIC B)

MEAS. 1—4. Partners join right hands, keeping free left hand on left hip. They do a step-balance forward on the right foot, and back on the left foot. This action is repeated.

MEAS. 5—8. Partners again join hands and circle left with eight steps. On the last count, each person drops hands and takes another step to his left, moving on to a new partner to begin the dance.

NOTE: In one version, the dance begins with three *claps*, followed by three stamps. This is less common than the way presented here. In Part Two, Meas. 1—4, a common variation is to have partners join right hands and do a step-swing balance, to the *right, left, right* and *left*, before circling left. This is a little more difficult than the action described here.

RECORDS: Folkraft 1159, RCA Victor LPM 1624, Educational Dance Recordings, FD-1.

# Come Let Us Be Joyful

This centuries-old dance expresses, in the words of Elizabeth Burchenal, the universal human need out of which folk dancing flowers the world over —"let us enjoy life." It is easy enough for young children, and is a pleasant dance for beginning adult folk dancers. The words are:

A. *Come let us be joyful, while life is bright and gay,*
*Gather its roses, ere they fade away.*
B. *We're always making our lives so blue, we look for thorns and find them too,*
*And leave the violets quite unseen, that bloom along the wayside.*

*Formation:* Sets of threes facing threes around the cricle, like spokes of a wheel (Diagram 10).

### Part One. (MUSIC A)

MEAS. 1—4. Each group of three, with inside hands joined and free hands on hips, walks forward three steps and bows to the opposite set of three (girls curtsey) on the fourth count. They then walk backward to place four steps.

MEAS. 5—8. Action of Meas. 1—4 is repeated.

### Part Two. (MUSIC B)

MEAS. 1—4. The center child turns with the partner on his right with a right elbow turn, *once*, with four skipping steps, and then turns the child on his left with a left elbow turn. As this is done, the child who is not being turned, turns about in place alone with four skips.

MEAS. 5—8. The action of Meas. 1—4 is repeated.

### Part Three. (MUSIC A)

MEAS. 1—4. The groups of three walk forward, bow, and backward to place, as in Part One, Meas. 1—4.

MEAS. 5—8. The threes drop hands, walk forward and pass through the opposite threes, each child passing right shoulders with the person opposite him. They now face a new group of three, and begin the dance again with them.

RECORDS: RCA Victor LPM 1622, Folkraft 1195, Educational Dance Recordings FD-1.

# Rig a Jig Jig

**∙∙∙∙∙∙∙∙∙∙∙∙∙∙∙∙∙∙∙∙∙∙∙∙∙∙∙∙∙∙∙∙∙∙∙∙∙∙∙∙∙∙∙∙∙∙** AMERICAN     GRADE THREE

This easy play party is an ideal dance for helping children choose partners, as part of a game-like mixer. Its words are:

A. *As I was walking down the street, down the street, down the street,*
   *As I was walking down the street, heigh-o, heigh-o, heigh-o.*
B. *A pretty girl I chanced to meet, chanced to meet, chanced to meet,*
   *A pretty girl I chanced to meet, heigh-o, heigh-o, heigh-o.*
C. *Rig a jig jig and away we go, away we go, away we go,*
   *Rig a jig jig and away we go, heigh-o, heigh-o, heigh-o.*

*Formation:* Children join hands in a single circle, without partners. One child stands in the circle, close to one side of it.

### Part One.

MEAS. 1—8. As the outer circle, with hands joined, walks sixteen steps to the left (clockwise) the inner child walks to the right (Verse A).

### Part Two.

MEAS. 1—8. This action is repeated in the opposite direction, with the circle going right, and the inner child left (Verse B). At the end of the verse, the child in the center picks a partner from the outer circle (boy choosing a girl, or vice-versa).

### Part Three.

MEAS. 1—8. The inner child and his new partner join hands in promenade position and skip sixteen steps counterclockwise around the inside of the circle, while the others clap hands, standing still (Verse C).

When the dance is repeated, the two children in the center separate and walk in single file to the right, while the outer circle goes to the left. When Part Three is done again they will each choose and promenade with a new partner, so the number of children in the center doubles each time.

RECORD: Folkraft 1415.

# Gustaf's Skoal

This simple square dance, in which the dancers pay homage to King Gustaf, is suitable both for children and adult beginners.

*Formation:* A square of four couples, each with its back parallel to a wall and at right angle to the other couples. The first couple has its back to the music or teacher's station; the others (two, three, four) are numbered off counter-clockwise. The *head* couples are One and Three. The *side* couples are Two and Four. Each boy's *partner* is the girl on his right. The girl on his left is his *corner.* (Diagram 12)

The words to the dance are:

A. *A toast we pledge, to Gustaf who is brave and true,*
   *A toast we pledge, to Gustaf brave and true.*
   *A toast we pledge, to Gustaf who is brave and true,*
   *A toast we pledge, to Gustaf brave and true.*
B. *Fa-la-la-la-la-la-la-la-la, Fa-la-la-la-la-la-la-la-la,*
   *Fa-la-la-la-la-la-la-la-la, Fa, la, la.*
   *Fa-la-la-la-la-la-la-la-la, Fa-la-la-la-la-la-la-la-la,*
   *Fa-la-la-la-la-la-la-la-la, Fa, la, la.*

### Part One. (MUSIC A)

MEAS. 1—4. With inside hands joined and free hands on waist, the head couples walk forward three steps singing the words. They bow deeply on the fourth count (on the word "pledge") and then walk backward four steps to place.

MEAS. 5—8. Side couples do action of Meas. 1—4.

MEAS. 1—8 (repeated). Action of Meas. 1—8 is repeated.

### Part Two. (MUSIC B)

MEAS. 1—8. As the side couples raise their joined inside hands to make arches, the head couples take four skips forward, release their partner's hands and turn away toward the arches (girl to right, boy to left). Holding the opposite person's hand briefly, they skip under the arch, release the hand, clap their own hands, and return to original places. Joining both hands with their partners, the head couples swing once around with four skipping steps. The entire action takes sixteen continuous skipping steps.

MEAS. 1—8 (*repeated*). The action of Meas. 9—16 is repeated, with the side couples active, and the head couples making the arches.

NOTE: The first part of the dance is done in a dignified manner; the second part is much more lively and free. Dancers around the room who do not have partners may "cut in" by quickly stepping into the set and swinging a partner during the second part of the dance—thus forcing a dancer out, who waits for his chance to "steal" as the dance is repeated.

RECORD: R. C. A. Victor LPM 1622; Folkraft 1175; Educational Dance Recordings FD-1.

## Green Sleeves

●●●●●●●●●●●●●●●●●●●●●●●●●●●●●●●●●●●●●●●●●● ENGLAND       GRADE FOUR

This is a spirited marching dance which all ages enjoy.

*Formation:* Double circle of two-couple sets, all facing counter-clockwise. Each girl is on her partner's right; inside hands are joined and outside hands are free at the side.

*Part One.* (MUSIC A)

MEAS. 1—8. All march forward with sixteen lively steps.

*Part Two.* (MUSIC B)

MEAS. 1—8. The couple in front turns to face the couple behind them, each person turning individually. They join right hands in a star and walk eight steps clockwise, then turn, join left hands, and walk eight steps counter-clockwise. On the last count, the leading couple turns to face forward again, in the beginning position.

*Part Three.* (MUSIC B)

MEAS. 1—8. The couple in back forms an arch by raising their joined inside hands, and walks forward four steps, while the leading couple backs under this arch, four steps. They reverse roles, with the couple now in front backing under, and the couple now in back making the arch and walking forward. This entire action is repeated. It is known as "turning the sleeves inside out."

NOTE: Young children may prefer to skip, rather than walk, throughout the entire dance.

RECORD: Methodist World of Fun Series MH 106; RCA Victor LPM 1624; Educational Dance Recordings, FD-1.

# Seven Jumps

•••••••••••••••••••••••••••••••••••••••••••••• DENMARK       GRADE FOUR

Originally a boys' and men's dance, this amusing novelty may be enjoyed by girls as well. It has a follow-the-leader kind of pattern, in which new actions are added each time the dance is done.

*Formation:* A single circle with hands joined; no partners needed.

*Chorus:* The chorus is done at the beginning, after each part of the dance, and again at the end.

(MUSIC A.)

MEAS. 1—8. With hands joined, all do seven vigorous step-hops to the left (leaning back to increase the momentum) and jump on both feet on the eighth count.

MEAS. 9—16. Repeat the action to the right. If children are too young to do the step-hop, they may skip or run.

*Part One.* Placing hands on hips, each person raises his right knee high on the first note of music. On the second note, he returns it to the floor. He waits on the third, *warning* note. Then do CHORUS.

*Part Two.* The right knee is lifted, then put down. The left knee is lifted and put down. Wait during the *warning* note. Then do CHORUS.

*Part Three.* Do each of the preceding actions: right knee, left knee; then kneel on right knee. Rise, wait, then do CHORUS.

*Part Four.* Do each of the previous actions, and add: kneel on left knee. Then rise, wait, do CHORUS.

*Part Five.* Do all previous actions and add: place right elbow on floor, resting chin on right hand. Then rise, wait, do CHORUS.

*Part Six.* Do all previous actions and add: place left elbow on floor, resting chin on left hand. Then rise, wait, do CHORUS.

*Part Seven.* Do previous actions and add: place forehead on floor. Then rise, wait, do final CHORUS.

NOTE: Each action should be held exactly as long as its musical note indicates.

RECORD: RCA Victor LPM 1623

# Cshebogar

This is a simplified version of a popular Hungarian circle dance, whose name means "the beetle."

**Formation:** Couples join hands in a single circle, facing in.

**Part One.** (MUSIC A)

MEAS. 1—4. Circle eight sliding steps to the left, two slides per measure. This may be done with seven slides and a jump.

MEAS. 5—8. Repeat this action to the right.

**Part Two.** (MUSIC A)

MEAS. 1—4. All take three steps forward, raising arms, and stamping on the fourth. Then take three steps backward, lowering arms, and stamping on the fourth count.

MEAS. 5—8. Partners face, join right elbows, and swing around eight skipping steps in place.

**Part Three.** (MUSIC B)

MEAS. 1—4. Partners face each other in a single circle, join hands with arms extended to the side, and take four slow step-draws (step-close) toward the center, moving to the boy's left and girl's right. The weight is not transferred on the last step. Arms go up and down with a rocking motion as this is done.

MEAS. 5—8. Each couple does four step-draws, away from the center, not transferring weight on the last step.

**Part Four.** (MUSIC B)

MEAS. 1—4. Each couple does two step-draws to the center, and two away, as before.

MEAS. 5—8. Again they hook elbows and swing with eight skips.

RECORDS: RCA Victor LPM 1624, Folkraft 1196, Educational Dance Recordings FD-1.

# *Bleking*

•••••••••••••••••••••••••••••••••••••••••• S W E D E N         GRADE FOUR

This lively dance makes use of a special step, called the "Bleking" step, named after a Swedish province. The same action is found in many folk dances of other lands.

*Formation:* Most descriptions refer to this as a single circle of couples, with partners facing each other. Some teachers will find it more convenient to have children form a double circle, boys with backs to the center.

*Part One.* (MUSIC A)

MEAS. 1. Joining hands with partners, children hop on the left foot thrusting the *right* foot forward, heel on the floor, toe up. At the same time, they sharply thrust the *right* hand forward. This is all done on the first count. On the second count, the *left* heel and hand are thrust forward.

MEAS. 2. The same action is done three times quickly, *right-left-right*, with a hold on the fourth count.

MEAS. 3—4. Repeat the action of Meas. 1—2, leading with the left foot, so the action is LEFT and RIGHT and left-right-left, hold.

MEAS. 5—8. Repeat action of Meas. 1—4.

*Part Two.* (MUSIC B)

MEAS. 1—8. Still holding hands with partners, children extend their arms straight out to the side. Starting with the boy's left foot and the girl's right, they do sixteen step-hops, turning clockwise as a couple and traveling counter-clockwise around the circle. This is done with a vigorous "rocking" side-to-side motion, like a windmill.

NOTE: In one variation of Part Two, they turn in place with eight step-hops to the left, and then eight to the right. If the turning step-hop is too difficult, children may join inside hands and do sixteen step-hops forward around the circle.

RECORD: RCA Victor LPM 1622, Folkraft 1188.

# *Lott' 1st Tod*

●●●●●●●●●●●●●●●●●●●●●●●●●●●●●●●●●●●●●●●●●●    S W E D E N          GRADE FOUR

Many versions of this dance are found throughout the Scandinavian and Baltic countries.

*Formation:* Double circle of couples in ballroom dance position, boys with backs to the center.

### *Part One.* (MUSIC A)

MEAS. 1—2. Couples take four slow slides (step-draws) to the boy's left and girl's right.

MEAS. 3—4. They slide in the opposite direction with eight quick slide steps.

MEAS. 5—8. Action of Meas. 1—4 is repeated.

### *Part Two.* (MUSIC B)

MEAS. 1—8. Couples do sixteen polka steps, turning and traveling counter-clockwise around the circle. If children are unable to do this, they may join inside hands and do forward, or face-to-face and back-to-back polka steps around the circle, or even skip.

NOTE: In one variation of the dance, there is a legend about a large rock on the Finnish island of Radiko, behind which all the spinsters or un-married girls of the village are hidden when strangers come by. Thus, in Part One, the boys take their partners' hands and "drag" them unwillingly toward the center of the circle (The Rock) with four slow steps, then slide out quickly with eight fast steps. This adds fun to the dance, if the girls really pull back.

RECORD: RCA Victor LPM 1622.

# Circassian Circle

Versions of this lively, simple mixer have also been found throughout the United States.

*Formation:* Single circle of couples with hands joined, facing the center.

*Part One.* (MUSIC A)

MEAS. 1—4. All walk four steps toward the center, bowing or curtseying on the fourth step, and then walk backward four steps to place.

MEAS. 5—8. This action is repeated.

MEAS. 1—4. Releasing hands, the girls walk forward, curtseying on the fourth step, and walk backward four steps to place.

MEAS. 5—8. The boys walk forward, bow, *turn,* and walk back to partner with four steps.

*Part Two.* (MUSIC B)

MEAS. 1—8. Each child joins both hands with his partner and swings with sixteen skipping or walking steps.

MEAS. 1—8. In promenade position, each couple walks sixteen steps around the circle, moving counter-clockwise. Face center, ready to begin again.

NOTE: When the boys return from the center, they may go to the girl on their *left* (corner girl) swing her, and promenade her as a new partner. The swing may also be done as a buzz step, by older children.

RECORD: Folkraft 1247; Methodist World of Fun M109 (Good Humor); Educational Dance Recordings FD-1.

# *Hora*

•••••••••••••••••••••••••••••••••••••••• ISRAEL GRADE FIVE

The Hora is the national dance of Israel, having been brought there from the Balkans. It is danced at many festive occasions to many traditional tunes, and is a symbol of national strength and spirit.

*Formation:* Dancers form a single circle, facing in, without partners. Hands may be joined, or may be extended along neighbors' arms, so elbows or shoulders are gripped.

## Version One

This is the simpler and better-known Hora. It is begun slowly and gradually speeded up.

MEAS. 1. Each dancer steps to the left side with his left foot, and then steps onto his right foot, crossing it behind the left.

MEAS. 2. The dancer steps to the left side with his left foot. Hopping on the left foot, he swings the right foot across in front of it.

MEAS. 3. He steps on the right foot in place and then, hopping on it, he swings the left foot across in front of it.

NOTE: In some versions, the Hora is done to the *right*. Actually, it may be done in either direction, and may have its direction reversed at any time after a brief interlude in which each dancer does this action in place: lightly *jump* (hold), *jump* (hold), and *jump-jump-jump*, (hold).

## Version Two

Dvora Lapson describes a slightly more difficult form of the Hora that is typical of some of the newer Israeli dances.

MEAS. 1. Each dancer steps to the left with the left foot and then cross the right foot *in front* of it.

MEAS. 2. He jumps lightly on both feet, with feet close together, and then hops on his left foot in place, lightly lifting the right foot.

MEAS. 3. He takes three quick steps (right-left-right) in place.

RECORDS: Folkraft 1110B; Folkraft 1116A; RCA Victor LPM 1623; Educational Dance Recordings, FD-2.

# La Raspa

La Raspa is a simple little novelty dance, based on a Mexican folk tune, and is not the traditional and difficult Mexican Hat Dance, with which it is sometimes confused. Sometimes teen-agers call it the "Mexican Shuffle," because of the appearance of the "Bleking" step in the first part.

*Formation:* Couples form a double circle, boys with backs to the center.

### Part One. (MUSIC A)

MEAS. 1—2. Holding hands, each child hops in place on the left foot, simultaneously thrusting the *right* foot and *right* arm sharply forward. The foot goes forward with a gliding step, close to the floor, and the toe is *not* pointed up. He then thrusts the *left* foot and arm forward, and again the *right* foot and arm. He "holds" for one count.

MEAS. 3—8. This action is repeated three times more, leading with alternating feet. From the beginning, the cue is: RIGHT-LEFT-RIGHT, hold, LEFT-RIGHT-LEFT, hold, RIGHT-LEFT-RIGHT, hold, LEFT-RIGHT-LEFT, hold. On some records, all of Part One may be repeated.

### Part Two. (MUSIC B)

MEAS. 1—4. Each child claps his own hands, hooks right elbows with his partner, and they skip around each other with eight steps. They clap hands, join left elbows, and skip around eight steps.

MEAS. 5—8. The action of Meas. 1—4 is repeated.

NOTE: There are several possible variations. In Part One, children sometimes clap their own hands quickly twice, on the count of "hold." In Part Two, children may skip sixteen steps with the right elbow and sixteen with the left. They may also join hands and skip in a circle to the left and right, or do a grand right and left around the circle, on this part.

RECORDS. Folkraft 1119, RCA Victor 1623, Methodist World of Fun MH106, Educational Dance Recordings, FD-1.

# Oh, Susanna

:::::::::::::::::::::::::::::::::::::::::::    AMERICAN        GRADE FIVE

This dance is very much like the Circassian Circle, but adds a new step, the *grand right and left*, which makes it a useful dance to learn before doing square dancing.

**Formation:** Single circle of couples, facing the center.

### Part One. (MUSIC A)

MEAS. 1—4. All the girls walk forward four steps to the center, clapping hands on the fourth step, and back up four steps to place.

MEAS. 5—8. All the boys walk forward, stamp on the fourth step, and back up four steps to place.

### Part Two.

MEAS. 1—8. Partners face each other and do a "grand right and left," by taking right hands and walking past (passing right shoulders), taking left hands with the next person and walking past (passing left shoulders) etc. This is continued until each person has met seven others—which should be the end of the verse of music.

### Part Three. (MUSIC B)

MEAS. 1—8. Each person meets a new partner and swings with a two-hand skipping or walk-around swing. Those who do not find a partner at once walk into the center and look for one.

### Part Four.

MEAS. 1—8. All promenade with sixteen walking steps, singing the chorus of the song.

NOTE: Older children may use a buzz swing, in Part Three.

RECORD: RCA Victor, LPM 1623; Educational Dance Recordings SG-2.

# Noriu Miego

Again we find the "Bleking" step, in a popular, easy Lithuanian dance.

*Formation:* Sets of two couples facing each other in a double circle, or scattered around the room. Girls have hands on hips, boys arms crossed in front of chest.

### Part One. (MUSIC A)

MEAS. 1—2. All hop lightly in place on the left foot, placing the *right* foot forward, toes up. Hop on the right foot, placing the *left* foot forward.

MEAS. 3—4. Repeat this action, twice as fast: *right-left-right-left.*

### Part Two. (MUSIC B)

MEAS. 1—4. Each child claps his own hands twice, makes a right hand star with the others (boys joining hands over the girls' hands) and all walk six quick steps in a clockwise direction.

MEAS. 1—4. As the music repeats, they clap hands twice again, join left hands, and walk counter-clockwise six steps.

NOTE: In some versions the music speeds up steadily; in others, the musicians may deliberately change the tempo of either part of the dance. In either case, the children must listen carefully and do the steps so they fit the music exactly. In one variation, the dancers may all stand in a large circle and during Part Two, clap twice, join hands and circle left and then clap twice and circle right. Of this version, Neva Boyd commented, "I got this from a Lithuanian group in Chicago. I saw three generations dancing in the same circle."

RECORD: RCA Victor LPM 1624, Educational Dance Recordings FD-1.

# Maitelitza

Performed to a Russian folk tune, the original source of this dance is not known. It is, however, a lively and enjoyable dance for children or adults.

*Formation:* Sets of threes, with inside hands joined, all facing counter-clockwise. (Diagram 9)

### Part One. (MUSIC A)

MEAS. 1—8. Each person stamps on the right foot and then hops on it, swinging the left foot lightly across in front. He then stamps on the left foot, swinging the right foot across. This entire action is repeated three times more, and each group of three moves forward (counter-clockwise) as it is done.

### Part Two. (MUSIC A)

MEAS. 1—8. All turn to face the center (making a quarter turn to the left). Each person joins hands with those now on his right and left sides, making three concentric circles. All take eight slide steps to the right (not transferring weight on the last slide) and eight back to the left.

### Part Three. (MUSIC B)

MEAS. 1—8. All turn to face counter-clockwise and join hands in original threes. The middle person in each set of three raises the hand of the person on his left in an arch, and the child on the right walks forward slowly, under the arch, and back to place with eight steps. On the last four, the center person turns under his arm, following him. This action is repeated with the center person making an arch with the child on his right, and the one on the left going forward, under the arch, and back to place.

NOTE: In Part Two, when three concentric circles are formed, they may slide eight steps in different directions (inner circle LEFT, middle circle RIGHT, outer circle LEFT) and then reverse for eight steps. Also in Part Two, another variation is to have each dancer stand in a line of three, one behind the other, while facing the center. The child closest to the center joins hands with his neighbors in a circle, but the child *behind* him places his hands on his shoulders. The outermost child places his hands on the middle child's shoulders (Diagram 27) and then all take eight slides to the right, and to the left.

RECORD: Educational Dance Recordings, FD-2.

**Diagram 27**

# Circle Dances
# Without Partners

..................................... **7**

THE FIRST DANCE formation believed to have been used by primitive man was the closed circle. According to anthropologists and dance historians, dances done in this formation symbolized tribal unity and were often performed as part of religious ritual. They are found today primarily in the Balkan nations of Europe, although a number of countries in other regions still have dances done in circles without partners.

Most of the dances presented in this chapter come from Yugoslavia, and are called Kolos. Yugoslavia, because of its long history of wars, invasions, and oppressions, and its blending of several major ethnic groups, has a rich culture of dance lore. Although many of the dances have lost their original religious or historical meanings, there are still thousands of village groups in Yugoslavia today that perform their traditional Kolos, as well as such magnificent touring companies as the Yugoslav State Company from Belgrade.

The footwork of the Kolo (as well as of the Bulgarian Horo, the Rumanian Hora, and other similar national

dances) ranges widely from very simple steps which are monotonously repeated over and over again until they have an almost hypnotic effect, to
much more complicated steps performed to intricate rhythms. The music
and mood of the dances ranges from the quiet, subdued, and languorous
to the fiery, fierce, and warlike—sometimes within a single dance.

Originally, most Kolos were performed by men. In the wealthier Moslem
communities, women did not dance at all in public. In poorer villages, they
did their own dances, apart from the men, and usually danced in restrained,
modest fashion. In Greek Orthodox communities, women were permitted
to join in those Kolos which were social in nature, but often had their own
sections or dancing groups. By contrast, in the Israeli dances (which are
quite similar to some of the Kolos, but which show a blending of Eastern
European and Arabic influences as well) girls and women join in freely
with the men, demonstrating their equal status as workers and even soldiers,
in the Israeli society.

These dances, when performed in folk dance classes or groups in the
United States today, are enjoyed by both sexes. Since no partners are required,
all may join in easily; the dances are therefore very useful in beginning recreational dance sessions. It may be necessary to substitute an easier pattern for
one of the more complicated steps of the dance; when this occurs, the class
should understand that a modification of the dance has been made. The
teacher may find it helpful to have students standing in lines all facing in one
direction, when teaching these circle dances. After they have learned the
steps, students should take the proper formation.

# Seljancica Kolo

●●●●●●●●●●●●●●●●●●●●●●●●●●●●●●●●●●●●●●●●●●● YUGOSLAVIA

Vyts Beliajus describes this dance, sometimes called the "Djacko" or Student Kolo, as one of the most popular of all the Kolos. Here is a somewhat simplified version of it.

*Formation:* Single circle facing in, hands joined, without partners. The circle may be broken at one point, with the dancer on the right leading the line around.

### Part One. (MUSIC A)

MEAS. 1—2. Each dancer steps with his right foot to the right, crosses with his left foot behind the right, and steps with the right foot to the side again. Hopping on the right foot, he lightly swings the left foot across in front.

MEAS. 3—4. Stepping with the left foot to the side, he crosses right foot behind the left, steps on the left foot again, hops on it, and lightly swings the right foot across in front.

MEAS. 5—8. The action of Meas. 1—4 is repeated.

### Part Two. (MUSIC B)

MEAS. 1—2. Each dancer steps on his right foot and hops on it, lightly swinging the left foot across in front. He steps on the left, swinging the right foot across.

MEAS. 3—4. The action of Meas. 1—2 is repeated.

### Part Three. (MUSIC C)

MEAS. 1—8. The circle takes eight light walking steps to the right, turns and takes eight light walking steps to the left.

NOTE: Each part of this dance may be done differently by more experienced dancers. Part One is actually a modification of the Basic Kolo Step which, when done correctly, is this:

1. Hop on the left foot, step in place on the right foot, cross the left foot behind the right, step in place on the right foot, and hop on the right foot.
2. Hop on the right foot, step in place on the left foot, cross the right foot behind, step in place on the left foot and hop on it.

In Part Two, instead of the step-swing, each dancer may do this in place: step right, bring left foot up to it, step left, bring right foot up to it. *Or*, he may take "threes" in place: right-left-right, left-right-left, etc.

Part Three may be done with what is called a "lame duck" step: traveling to the right, hop on left foot, place right heel forward, bring right foot back, placing weight on the ball of the foot, and step forward with the left foot. This is done very quickly and is difficult for inexperienced dancers.

Throughout the Kolo, the action should be done with short, bouncy steps, close to the floor, with flexed knees.

RECORD: Folk Dancer MH-1006; Educational Dance Recordings FD-2.

## *Nebesko Kolo*

•••••••••••••••••••••••••••••••••••••••••• YUGOSLAVIA

The name of this fast-moving Serbian Kolo means "heavenly circle."

*Formation:* Single circle, without partners, facing center with hands joined.

### Part One. (MUSIC A)

MEAS. 1—4. Starting with the right foot, each dancer does four two-steps to his right. He turns in the reverse direction on the last count, still holding hands.

MEAS. 5—8. Each dancer now does four two-steps to the left. On the last count, he faces the center.

### Part Two. (MUSIC B)

MEAS. 1—2. Each dancer steps forward on his right foot and then rocks back on the left foot (in effect, keeping it in place). He steps backward on the right foot and again steps on the left foot in place. This is done rapidly: right-left-right-left; each foot takes the weight for a moment.

MEAS. 3—4. The action of Meas. 1—2 is repeated.

### Part Three. (MUSIC B)

MEAS. 1—4. Each dancer does the pas de bas (see page 31) to his right and then to his left. He repeats this, to the right, and to the left, and finally ends with a sharp stamp with the right foot in place. The foot is then lifted to begin the dance.

NOTE: A variation of Part One is to travel to the right with two running two-steps (right and left) two low, diagonal leaps (right and left) and three quick steps (right-left-right), turning to repeat the action to the left, starting with the left foot.

RECORD: Balkan 513; Folk Dancer MH-1003; Educational Dance Recordings FD-4.

# Cherkassiya

Dvora Lapson describes this as a dance for men, originating with Mohammedan tribesmen who, seeking freedom, went to Palestine and Syria from Russia at the end of the 19th Century. Other authorities claim they were of the Christian faith, but all are agreed that they were expert horsemen, and that this dance suggests the movements of the horses and their riders. While the dance may seem long and complicated at first glance, it is quite easy to do, and most enjoyable, even for beginning dancers.

*Formation:* This dance may be done in facing lines of dancers. The commoner formation today is a single circle facing in, with hands joined, or arms extended behind neighbors' back, gripping hands of the next neighbors.

### Chorus. (MUSIC A)

MEAS. 1—2. A grapevine step, in which each dancer crosses with his right foot in front of his left with a stamp, and taking the weight. He then takes a very short step to the left side with the left foot. He crosses with the right foot behind the left, taking the weight, and again takes a short side step with the left foot.

MEAS. 3—8. The action of Meas. 1—2 is repeated three times more. The entire CHORUS is done following each part of the dance.

### Part One. (MUSIC B)

MEAS. 1—8. Each dancer steps to the right with his right foot, with the left foot extended to the side. He crosses his left foot behind the right, taking the weight, and bending both knees slightly. This is done quickly, almost as a running step, eight full times, traveling to the right. Repeat CHORUS.

### Part Two. (MUSIC B)

MEAS. 1—8. The "horse trot." All face to the right and do eight step-hops, leading with the right foot. Repeat CHORUS.

### Part Three. (MUSIC B)

MEAS. 1—8. In American terminology, the "Suzie-Q." Keeping both feet together, each dancer moves his toes to the right and then, without lifting his feet, moves his heels to the right. This is done continuously, eight times. Repeat CHORUS.

### Part Four. (MUSIC B)

MEAS. 1—8. "Scissors forward." In place, beginning with the right foot, each dancer kicks his feet forward sixteen times, alternating them (right, left, right, left, etc.) Repeat CHORUS.

**Part Five.** (MUSIC B)

MEAS. 1—8. "Scissors backward." Same action as Part Four, kicking feet backward in place. Repeat CHORUS.

**Part Six.** (MUSIC B)

MEAS. 1—8. "The train." All face to the right and bending knees but with trunk of body erect, take fourteen walking steps counter-clockwise. End with a high jump on both feet, facing the center.

RECORDS: Israel Music Foundation 116B; RCA Victor LPM 1623; Educational Dance Recordings FD-3.


# *Milanovo Kolo*

••••••••••••••••••••••••••••••••••••••••• YUGOSLAVIA

Another simple, spirited Kolo, said to be popular among Serbs in the Pittsburgh area. It is named after Milan, a man's name, rather than the Italian city.

**Formation:** Single circle without partners, facing in, hands joined.

**Part One.** (MUSIC A)

MEAS. 1. Beginning with the right foot and facing to the right, each dancer does two step-hops: right-hop, left-hop.

MEAS. 2. Facing the center, he steps to the right with the right foot, crosses his left foot behind, and takes three quick steps in place: right-left-right.

MEAS. 3—4. The same action is done to the left, starting with the left foot: left-hop, right-hop, step to the left, cross right behind and three quick steps: left-right-left.

**Part Two.** (MUSIC B)

MEAS. 1—2. Facing the center and bringing arms up so they are extended forward at shoulder height, each dancer moves forward with three steps: right-left-right, and pause, and, continuing forward, left-right-left, and pause.

MEAS. 3—4. The same action is done backward: right-left-right, pause, and left-right-left, pause. Arms are lowered.

RECORD: RCA Victor LPM 1620; Stanchel 1011-B.

# Jibidi, Jibida

This amusing little dance may be done in a circle without partners, or *with* partners. It is easy enough for children, and adult beginners will enjoy it as well.

*Formation:* A single circle, with hands joined, facing center.

*Part One.* (MUSIC A)

MEAS. 1—2. All step sideward to the left with the left foot. Close right foot to it, taking the weight. Repeat this, stepping sideward with the left, and closing with the right.

MEAS. 3—4. Swing the left foot forward and back (bending the right knee slightly). Stamp in place with the left foot and pause.

MEAS. 5—8. Repeat action of Meas. 1—4.

*Part Two.* (MUSIC B)

MEAS. 1—2. With hands still joined, spring lightly in place on the left foot, placing the right foot forward, heel on floor, toe pointing up. Spring on right foot in place, putting left foot forward, toe up.

MEAS. 3—4. Do this action quickly three times, placing the right, left and right foot forward.

MEAS. 5—8. Repeat action of Meas. 1—4: left, right, and left, right, left.

NOTE: In her original version of the dance, Elizabeth Burchenal included only the above steps. Michael Herman suggests another action: if couples are dancing, they may face each other and, as they spring with the right foot forward, shake right forefingers, and with the left foot forward, left forefingers. This version would alternate with Part Two as described above.

The following nonsense syllables may be sung during the dance.

A. *Tra la la la la la la la la, tra la la la la la la la,*
   *Tra la la la la la la la, tra la la la la la la.*

B. *Ji-bi-di, Ji-bi-da, tra la la la la la la!*
   *Ji-bi-di, Ji-bi-da, tra la la la la la la!*

RECORD: Folk Dancer MH-1044.

# *Tropanka*

This lively dance is not too complicated. It has so much stamping that it is sometimes called the "stamping dance."

*Formation:* Single circle, facing center, without partners. Hands joined.

### *Part One.* (MUSIC A)

MEAS. 1—2. Beginning with the right foot, all take five quick steps to the right, ending with the weight on the right foot. Stamp twice with the left foot, with the toe turned out slightly. Pause for one count.

MEAS. 3—4. Repeat this action to the left, taking five steps and stamping twice with the right foot.

MEAS. 5—8. Repeat this entire action.

### *Part Two.* (MUSIC B)

MEAS. 1—2. Facing the center, step and hop on the right foot, swinging the left foot across lightly in front. Step and hop on the left foot, swinging the right foot across. Then step on the right foot in place and stamp the left foot twice. Pause for one count.

MEAS. 3—4. Do the same action, stepping on the left foot, hopping and swinging the right foot over: step-hop swing, step-hop swing, step, stamp-stamp.

MEAS. 5—8. Repeat this entire action.

### *Part Three.* (MUSIC C)

MEAS. 1—2. Starting with the right foot, do two-step hops forward, toward the center: RIGHT-hop, LEFT-hop. Then step on the right foot and stamp the left foot twice. As this is done, hands are brought up, and the dancers shout "Hey!"

MEAS. 3—4. This action is repeated moving backward, starting with the left foot and lowering arms: LEFT-hop, RIGHT-hop, step (left), stamp-stamp.

MEAS. 5—8. This entire action is repeated.

RECORD: Folk Dancer MH-1020.

# Lech Lamidbar

This fast-moving circle dance, "Let's Go To The Desert," was originated in the Israeli army and has become widely popular both in that nation and in American folk dance groups.

*Formation:* Single circle without partners, facing the center, with hands joined, arms down.

### Part One. (MUSIC A)

MEAS. 1—2. All leap to the right with the right foot. Cross the left foot over in front of the right, taking the weight on it. Step on the right foot in place and hold for one count. Take two small step-draws to the left, not taking the weight on the right foot on the last count.

MEAS. 3—8. Repeat action of Meas. 1—2, three more times.

### Part Two. (MUSIC B)

MEAS. 1—2. In place, step-hop on right foot and lightly kick the left foot forward. Step-hop on the left foot and lightly kick the right foot forward. Do two grapevine steps to the left (as in the CHORUS of Cherkassiya), crossing the right foot in front, stepping with the left foot slightly to the side, crossing the right foot behind, and again stepping with the left foot slightly to the side.

MEAS. 3—8. Repeat action of Meas. 1—2, three more times.

### Part Three. (MUSIC A)

MEAS. 1—2. Step directly forward on the right foot, bringing joined hands sharply up. Hold one count, step back on left foot (lowering hands) and close right foot to left. Take two step-draws to left, without taking the weight on the right foot on the last count.

MEAS. 3—4. Repeat action of Meas. 1—2.

### Part Four

MEAS. 5—8. Do four grapevine steps to left: cross RIGHT in front, LEFT to side, RIGHT in back, LEFT to side, RIGHT in front, LEFT to side, RIGHT in back and hop on the right foot, freeing the left. Do this same action in reverse: cross LEFT in front, RIGHT to side, LEFT in back, RIGHT to side, LEFT in front, RIGHT to side, LEFT in back, and hop on LEFT, freeing the right.

MEAS. 5—8. (Repeated). Repeat action of Meas. 5—8.

NOTE: In the dance, as described by Dvora Lapson, Part Three is done with two balance steps (to the right and to the left), and *then* the forward and back step. In Part Four, instead of simply doing a step-hop at the end of each grapevine sequence, she has the dancer jump lightly onto both feet and then hop on the supporting foot lifting the free foot (first left, then right) to begin the grapevine again.

RECORD: Folk Dancer MH-1093A; Israel Music Foundation 118B.

# Ersko Kolo

•••••••••••••••••••••••••••••••••••••••   YUGOSLAVIA

This is one of the easiest of the Kolos, performed to a catchy melody that soon has the dancers humming it!

*Formation:* Single circle without partners, facing the center. Hands are joined, with arms down at sides. Each dancer stands proudly erect.

### Part One. (MUSIC A)

MEAS. 1—8. The circle travels to the right as each dancer places his right foot to the side (weight on the heel), and then crosses his left foot behind the right, taking the weight. This is done fourteen times to the right, moving slowly (on the accented beats). Then each dancer stamps with his right foot and then his left in place, lifting the left foot slightly.

MUSIC A

MEAS. 1—8. The same action is done to the left, fourteen times, stepping to the side with the left and crossing with the right behind. Then two slow stamps, left and right. The right foot is lifted slightly and each dancer faces to the right.

### Part Two. (MUSIC B)

MEAS. 1—4. Each dancer does a forward schottische to the right (counter-clockwise), right-left-right, hop; and a backward schottische (clockwise) left-right-left, hop. Facing the center, he again does a forward schottische: right-left-right, hop, and a backward schottische: left-right-left, hop.

MEAS. 5—8. The action of Meas. 1—4 is repeated.

RECORD: Folk Dancer MH-3020.

# Kuma Echa

•••••••••••••••••••••••••••••••••••••••••••••  ISRAEL

Vyts Beliajus has described an older version of this dance in his book "Dance and Be Merry." This spirited version was composed more recently, based on a folk melody and familiar folk steps; it has gained wide popularity among folk dancers.

*Formation:* Circle without partners, hands joined facing center.

### Part One. (MUSIC A)

MEAS. 1—2. All take three running steps into the center of the circle, starting with the right foot: right-left-right, and hop on the right. Each dancer leans forward and raises his head and arms as he travels forward. The same action is done backward: left-right-left, and hop on the left foot, freeing the right foot. The arms are lowered.

MEAS. 3—4. Each dancer does two grapevine steps to his left, crossing the right foot over in front of the left and placing his weight on it, stepping with the left foot to the side slightly, crossing the right foot behind, and taking a little leap onto the left foot. This action is repeated.

MEAS. 5—8. The entire action of Meas. 1—4 is repeated. At the end, the right foot is closed to the left, but does not take the weight.

### Part Two. (MUSIC B)

MEAS. 1. The circle moves to the right as each dancer turns in this direction and runs: right and left. He twists his body to the left and continues to travel in the *same* direction, running backward: right and left.

MEAS. 2—4. The running action of Meas. 1 is continued, three times more.

MEAS. 5. Each dancer runs forward, to the center, with four steps: right-left-right-left.

MEAS. 6—8. Each dancer stamps on his right foot, letting it take the weight, steps in place on the left foot, steps backward on the right foot, and in place on the left. This is done three times altogether, as the circle slowly moves backward, away from the center. As the stamp is done each time, the joined hands are thrust forward and the dancers lean forward; on the steps backward, the arms are brought back and the dancers straighten up.

RECORDS: Folk Dancer MH-1150; Folkraft 1431; Educational Dance Recordings FD-4.

# *Alunelul*

●●●●●●●●●●●●●●●●●●●●●●●●●●●●●●●●●●●●●●●●●●● RUMANIA

The action of this dance is somewhat like the Bulgarian Tropanka, except that it has a "count-down" effect. In each succeeding part of the dance, the number of steps is reduced! This version was introduced by Larisa Lucaci at Folk Dance House, the Hermans' dance center in New York City, and by Dick Crum at Folk Dance Camp in Stockton, California.

*Formation:* A single circle without partners, facing in, arms on neighbors' shoulders.

### *Part One.* (MUSIC A)

MEAS. 1—2. Starting with the right foot, travel to the right: step RIGHT, cross behind with the LEFT, step RIGHT, cross behind with the LEFT, step RIGHT, and stamp twice with the LEFT. Pause.

MEAS. 3—4. Do this same action to the left, taking five steps, starting with the left, and stamp the right foot twice.

MEAS. 5—8. Repeat action of Meas. 1—4.

### *Part Two.* (MUSIC B)

MEAS. 1—2. Step to the right, with the RIGHT, cross behind with the LEFT, step again with the RIGHT, and stamp the LEFT foot once. Repeat this to the left, stepping LEFT, behind with the RIGHT, LEFT again, and stamping the RIGHT foot once.

MEAS. 3—4. Repeat the action of Meas. 1—2.

### *Part Three.* (MUSIC B)

MEAS. 1—2. In place step RIGHT, stamp LEFT; step LEFT, stamp RIGHT; step RIGHT, stamp LEFT twice. Do this in the reverse direction: step LEFT, stamp RIGHT; step RIGHT, stamp LEFT; step LEFT; stamp RIGHT twice.

MEAS. 3—4. Repeat the action of Meas 1—2.

RECORD: Folk Dancer MH-1120; Elektra EKL-206.

# Misirlou

•••••••••••••••••••••••••••••••••••••••••••  GREEK-AMERICAN

Probably the best known of all the dances in this chapter, this dance is based on the Greek dance Kritikos. Its music has a haunting quality.

*Formation:* A broken circle facing in, without partners. Each dancer may link little fingers with his neighbors, or may hold the end of a scarf or handkerchief.

### Part One.

MEAS. 1. Facing the center, all step slightly forward and to the side on the right foot and hold one count. Touch the left toe forward in front of the right, without placing the weight on it. Pause again.

MEAS. 2. Sweep the left foot around in an arc, to the left side and behind the right, placing the weight on it. Step with the right foot to the side and cross the left foot in front of the right, taking the weight. This is done in three quick steps. Hold for one count, and during this count pivot (without changing weight) on the left foot, to face directly to the left.

MEAS. 3. Take three forward steps, right-left-right, in this direction (clockwise). Hold on the fourth count, lifting the left foot slightly.

MEAS. 4. Take three backward steps, left-right-left (counter-clockwise). Hold on the fourth count, lifting the right foot slightly and turning to face the center.

NOTE: A helpful set of cues is: step RIGHT, touch LEFT, cross BEHIND-two-three, turn; RIGHT-left-right, hold, LEFT-right-left, hold.

RECORD: Columbia 10072; RCA Victor LPM 1620; Educational Dance Recordings FD-3; Elektra EKL-206.

# Couple Dances

........................................ *8*

*THIS CHAPTER INCLUDES* twenty-five couple dances of fourteen nationalities. They are all "independent" dances, in that each couple moves freely around the floor, usually in a counter-clockwise direction. They are grouped according to the dance step they are based on (schottische, waltz, two-step or polka, and mazurka) and, within each category, are placed in approximate order of difficulty.

Most of these dances tend to be of fairly recent origin— within the last century or two. They are social, rather than ritual or ceremonial in derivation. In fact, quite a number of them are round dances, or ballroom dances of the last century. Because they are based on such steps as the two-step, schottische, or waltz, and because they have a unique flavor and charm that is quite different from the ballroom dances of today, they may almost be considered folk dances.

Often, too, because they require less physical effort than other dances done in the circle or square formations, they are especially appropriate for older dancers. Taken as a whole, they represent some of the most popular dances done in school and community recreation folk dance classes today.

# Road to the Isles

•••••••••••••••••••••••••••••••••••••••••• SCOTLAND

Based on the schottische, this simple little couple dance is done to a favorite marching melody of the Scottish pipe bands.

*Formation:* Couples facing to the right, in Varsovienne position.

### Part One. (MUSIC A)

MEAS. 1. Point the left toe diagonally forward and to the left, and hold. (Footwork is same for both man and lady.)

MEAS. 2—3. Cross with the left foot behind the right, step with the right foot to the right, and cross with the left foot in front of the right, taking the weight. Hold one count.

MEAS. 4. Point the right toe diagonally forward and to the right, and hold.

MEAS. 5—6. Cross with the right foot behind the left, with the left foot to the left, and cross with the right foot in front of the left, taking the weight. Hold one count.

MEAS. 7—8. Lightly touch the left toe forward, hold, and then touch it backward, keeping the weight on the right. Hold one count.

### Part Two. (MUSIC B)

MEAS. 1—4. Beginning with the left foot, take two schottische steps forward, moving counter-clockwise: left-right-left-hop, right-left-right-hop. On the last hop, each person takes a right-face turn in place, keeping hands joined at shoulder height. The couple now faces clockwise, and lady is on her partner's left.

MEAS. 5—6. Take one schottische in the clockwise direction, left-right-left-hop. On the hop, take a left-face turn, and face in original direction.

MEAS. 7—8. Take three light steps forward: right, left, right.

RECORD: Imperial 1005A; Folk Dancer MH-3003; Educational Dance Recordings FD-2; Elektra EKL-206.

# *Korobushka*

This dance, performed to a favorite old Russian folk song about a "pedlar's pack," was supposedly originated in the United States by a group of Russian immigrants shortly after World War I.

*Formation:* Double circle of couples, men with backs to center. Partners join both hands.

### *Part One.* (MUSIC A)

MEAS. 1. Beginning with his left foot, man does schottische forward (away from center of circle) as lady, beginning with her right foot, does a schottische backward.

MEAS. 2. Beginning with his right foot, each man does a schottische backward (toward the center), as lady moves forward, starting left.

MEAS. 3. Repeat action of Meas. 1. Man's right foot is now free, and lady's left.

MEAS. 4. Man hops on his left foot, touching right toe across in front; hops again on left, touching right toe out to right side; hops again on left and brings feet together. This is called the "bo-kaz-ni," or Hungarian break step. Lady does opposite footwork, hopping on her right foot and crossing the left foot over, to the side and together.

### *Part Two.* (MUSIC B)

MEAS. 1. Releasing hands, both man and lady do one schottische step to their own right side, leading with the right foot and moving apart from each other.

MEAS. 2. Leading with the left foot, they do one schottische step to the left, returning to each other.

MEAS. 3. Joining right hands, partners balance forward on the right foot and back on the left.

MEAS. 4. Still holding right hands, partners change places with four walking steps, starting right. As they cross over, the lady does a left-face turn under the joined hands.

MEAS. 5—8. The man is now on the outside and the lady on the inside of the circle. They repeat the action of Meas. 1—4, doing a schottische to the right (apart), to the left (together), balancing forward and back, and crossing over to original positions.

RECORD: Folk Dancer MH-1059; Educational Dance Recordings FD-3; Elektra EKL-206.

# Meitschi Putz Di

Based on several traditional schottische figures, this Swiss dance is fairly challenging, and makes a good exhibition number.

*Formation:* Double circle of couples, men with backs to center, facing partners.

### Chorus. (MUSIC A)

MEAS. 1—2. Swinging joined right hands in an arc, down and then up, man steps to the left with his left foot, brings his right foot to it, stamps lightly, and bows. Lady does the same, leading with her right foot, and curtseys. Action is repeated in opposite direction.

MEAS. 3—4. Moving in line of direction, lady twirls with a right-face turn, with four step-hops under the joined right hands, as the man follows her with four forward step-hops.

MEAS. 5—6. Partners link right elbows and reach behind their backs with the free hand to grasp the other dancer's extended hand. They do four step-hops turning clockwise.

MEAS. 7—8. In original positions, with man facing counter-clockwise and lady clockwise, they clap their own knees once, hold, their own hands once, hold, turn to face each other and clap both hands against each other, three times.

### Part One. (MUSIC B)

MEAS. 1—2. Partners face and hold each other's arms above the elbow. Moving sidewards, they do a schottische to the man's left, and then to the man's right (lady does counterpart throughout).

MEAS. 3—4. With same arm position, they turn twice clockwise with four step-hops.

MEAS. 5—8. Repeat action of Meas. 1—4. There is a musical interlude, during which they bow or curtsey, and then do CHORUS.

### Part Two. (MUSIC B)

MEAS. 1—2. With inside hands joined and free hands on waist, each couple does two schottische steps forward (beginning with man's left, lady's right foot).

MEAS. 3—4. Man drops to kneel on his right knee as lady travels forward around him, counter-clockwise, with four step-hops, keeping inside hands joined.

MEAS. 5—8. Repeat action of Meas. 1—4, except that in the second part, the lady drops to her left knee and the man step-hops around her. Musical interlude, and repeat CHORUS.

### Part Three. (MUSIC A)

MEAS. 1—4. Couples do a "diamond" schottische, with hands on waist. They do a schottische away from each other and then together, moving forward around the circle. In shoulder-waist position they turn twice clockwise with four step-hops.

MEAS. 5—8. Repeat action of Meas. 1—4.
Musical interlude and repeat CHORUS.
NOTE: The entire dance is done twice. At end, it is customary for man to "lift" his partner high in the air as she springs, with hands on his shoulders.
RECORD: Folk Dancer MH-1017A; Educational Dance Recordings FD-4.

# To Ting

•••••••••••••••••••••••••••••••••••••••••• DENMARK

The name of this dance means "two things," and describes the two different kinds of action found in it.

**Formation:** Couples facing counter-clockwise in a double circle, in open position (inside hands joined, free hands on waist).

### Part One. (MUSIC A)

MEAS. 1—2. Traveling forward, each couple does two open waltz steps. Man begins with left foot and lady with right, as they turn away (swinging joined hands forward), and together (swinging joined hands back).

MEAS. 3—4. Action of Meas. 1—2 is repeated.

MEAS. 5—8. In closed dance position, they do four waltz steps, turning clockwise and moving in the line of direction.

MEAS. 1—8 (Repeated). Action of Meas. 1—8 is repeated.

### Part Two. (MUSIC B)

MEAS. 1—4. Each couple takes a "conversation" position: man's right arm around the lady's waist, her left hand on his right shoulder, and free hands on waist (Diagram 20). Beginning with the outside foot, they walk four steps forward.

MEAS. 5—8. Taking shoulder-waist position, they turn clockwise with four walking steps.

MEAS. 1—8 (Repeated). Repeat action of Meas. 1—8.
RECORD: Folk Dancer MH-1018; Educational Dance Recordings FD-2.

# Spinning Waltz

This easy and graceful Finnish waltz has a step pattern that has been imitated in many modern couple dances.

*Formation:* Couples in a double circle, men with backs to center, facing partners. Both hands are joined.

### Part One. (MUSIC A)

MEAS. 1—2. Man steps on left foot and swings right foot across in front lightly, then steps on right foot in place, swinging left foot across.

Lady does counterpart, starting by stepping on right and swinging left.

MEAS. 3—4. Continuing to hold the lady's right and man's left hand, the man does two step-draw steps to his left, *not* taking the weight on his left foot on the second step. Meanwhile the lady does a right-face turn under the joined hands, starting with the right foot, taking five steps and lightly swinging the left foot across in front of the right on the last step.

MEAS. 5—8. The same action is done in the reverse direction: step-swing, step-swing, and then the *lady* takes two step-draws to her left, as the *man* turns clockwise under the joined hands (his right, her left).

### Part Two. (MUSIC B)

MEAS. 1—2. In closed position, but turning slightly to face counter-clockwise, each person does two step-draws forward, leading with the outside foot. The weight is not transferred to the inside foot on the second step-draw.

MEAS. 3—4. They do the same action backward, leading with the inside foot.

MEAS. 5—8. In closed position, each couple does four waltz steps, turning clockwise and moving forward around the circle.

RECORD: Imperial 1036; World of Fun M110.

# *At the Inn*

A vigorous and happy dance, done to a German folk song, "Catherine's Wedding," which tells the story of the wedding celebration at the inn called "To The Crown."

*Formation:* Couples in double circle, men with backs to center.

### *Part One.* (MUSIC A)

MEAS. 1—4. Each person claps his own hands, claps right hands with his partner, claps left hands with his partner, and claps his own again.

MEAS. 5—8. Joining hands with arms extended at shoulder height, the couple turns once, clockwise, with four step-hops, beginning with the left foot. Dancers shout enthusiastically during this.

MEAS. 1—8. Repeat action of Meas. 1—8.

### *Part Two.* (MUSIC B)

MEAS. 1—4. With right hands joined overhead, lady turns clockwise with four waltz steps, moving counter-clockwise, as man follows her with four forward waltz steps.

MEAS. 5—8. In closed dance position, each couple does four turning waltz steps, moving counter-clockwise.

MEAS. 1—8. Repeat action of Meas. 1—8.

### *Part Three.* (MUSIC C)

MEAS. 1—4. In open position, with inside hands joined and free hands on waist, each couples moves forward with two waltz steps (starting with outside feet), balancing apart and together. Releasing hands, they turn completely away from each other, man to left, lady to right, in two waltz steps, still moving forward around circle.

MEAS. 5—8. Repeat action of Meas. 1—4, except that at end, each person turns halfway around, so the couple now faces in the opposite direction (clockwise).

MEAS. 1—4. Joining the new inside hands and starting with the outside feet, they do two forward, open waltzes, balancing apart and together, and then turning away with two waltzes.

MEAS. 5—8. This action is repeated, still moving clockwise around the circle. At the end, partners face each other, ready to repeat the dance.

RECORD: Folk Dancer MH-1022.

# St. Bernard's Waltz

•••••••••••••••••••••••••••••••••••••••••• ENGLAND

This lively waltz, of recent origin, is done to a catchy tune and is seen in both England and Scotland.

*Formation:* Couples in double circle, men with backs to center, in closed position.

### Part One

MEAS. 1—2. Moving to the side, counter-clockwise, each couple does two step-draws, leading with the man's left and lady's right.

MEAS. 3—4. Man steps with his left foot to the left, holds, and lightly stamps his right foot twice, as lady does counterpart.

MEAS. 5—6. Each couple now does two step-draws to the man's right and lady's left, *not* taking the weight with the following foot on the last step.

MEAS. 7—8. Man does two slow steps backward, toward center of circle, left and right, as lady steps forward, right and left.

MEAS. 9—10. The action of Meas. 7—8 is reversed, as man steps forward, left and right, with lady stepping backward, right and left.

MEAS. 11—12. With leading hands joined overhead (man's left, lady's right), the man takes two step-draws to his left, as the lady does a right face turn in six steps, moving in the line of direction.

MEAS. 13—16. Resuming closed position, each couple turns twice with four waltz steps, moving in the line of direction.

RECORD: Folkraft 1162; Educational Dance Recordings FD-3.

# Jessie Polka

This catchy little dance comes from the American Southwest. Its basic step is a two-step, rather than a polka.

*Formation:* The dance is done with groups of two or more dancers with arms around each other's waists traveling like spokes of a wheel counter-clockwise around the floor.

MEAS. 1. Place left heel diagonally forward, toe pointing up. Then step on left foot in place.

MEAS. 2. Keeping weight on left foot, touch right toe in back. Touch right toe lightly to floor in place, without taking weight.

MEAS. 3. Still keeping weight on left, touch right heel diagonally forward. Then step on right foot in place.

MEAS. 4. Touch left heel diagonally forward, and bring it back across and in front of the right foot, touching the left toe in front.

MEAS. 5—8. Four forward two-steps, beginning left, in line of direction.

NOTE: As the first part is done, when the left foot is placed forward, the dancer leans back. When the right foot is placed back, he leans forward. This adds fun to the dance.

RECORD: Capitol 3085 (A and E Rag); Educational Dance Recordings FD-2.

# Alexandrovsky

A subtle and graceful old Russian ballroom dance, probably named for one of the Czars.

**Formation:** Double circle of couples, partners facing with both hands joined, arms slightly extended at shoulder height.

### Part One. (MUSIC A)

MEAS. 1. Releasing man's left and lady's right hand, but keeping inside hands joined, each dancer takes three steps forward in the line of direction. At the same time, the joined hands are brought forward and outside hands stretched back at shoulder height, so partners are back to back.

MEAS. 2—4. In this position (Diagram 28), they do three step-draws forward, leading with the inside foot, and not transferring the weight to the outside foot on the last step.

*Diagram* 28

MEAS. 5—8. Reverse the action of Meas. 1—4. Starting with the outside foot, take three steps backward, swinging the joined hands back, and turning so partners are face to face. In this position take three step-draws to man's right (clockwise). Do not transfer weight to following foot on last step-draw.

MEAS. 1—8. Repeat action of Meas. 1—8.

### Part Two. (MUSIC A)

MEAS. 1—4. Releasing hands and extending them gracefully to the side, each dancer turns away with a complete turn in the line of direction (man to left, lady to right), with six walking steps. Facing each other, they do two step-draws in the line of direction, not transferring weight on the last step-draw.

MEAS. 5—8. Repeat this action in reverse direction, man turning to right and lady to left with six walking steps and doing two step-draws moving clockwise around circle.

MEAS. 1—8. Repeat action of Meas. 1—8.

### Part Three. (MUSIC A)

MEAS. 1—2. In promenade position, with arms crossed in front, and leading with the outside foot, walk six steps in the line of direction, turning toward each other after the third step (keeping hands joined) and traveling backward around the circle.

MEAS. 3—4. In this position take two draw steps backward, leading with the inside foot, and not transferring the weight the second time.

MEAS. 5—8. Repeat this action in the reverse direction: take six steps forward (clockwise) leading with outside foot, and turning toward partner on the fourth count to face counter-clockwise again, and then doing two draw steps backward.

MEAS. 1—8. Repeat action of Meas. 1—8.

### Part Four. (MUSIC A)

MEAS. 1—8 (Repeated). In ballroom dance position, do sixteen waltz steps, turning clockwise and moving counter-clockwise around the floor.

The entire dance is then repeated from the beginning.

NOTE: The sequences referred to as six walking steps are actually two running waltzes, with a slight accent on the first step of each measure.

RECORD: Folk Dancer MH-1057.

# Oxford Minuet

••••••••••••••••••••••••••••••••••••••• UNITED STATES

This old round dance has two parts: a dignified, slow action, almost like the minuet, and a bouncy, fast-turning two-step sequence which follows.

*Formation:* Couples in a double circle, lady on right of man in open position (inside hands joined, outside hands on waist, or lady's free hand holding her skirt). Both face counter-clockwise.

### Part One. (MUSIC A)

MEAS. 1. Leading with the outside foot (man's left, lady's right) both walk forward with three steps, and lightly touch the inside foot forward, without taking weight.

MEAS. 2. Leading with inside foot, take three walking steps, and touch outside foot to floor.

MEAS. 3. Partners face and join both hands. As lady does opposite foot-work, man steps on his left foot to the left, touching the right toe across in front, then steps on his right foot to the right and touches the left foot across in front.

MEAS. 4. Holding the lady's right hand overhead in his left, the man takes two step-draws to his left (not taking the weight on the right foot at the end) as the lady turns under the hand with a right-face turn, also traveling counter-clockwise.

MEAS. 5—8. The same action is done in the opposite direction, moving clockwise. Starting with the outside foot: walk-two-three, touch, walk-two-three, touch; step-touch, step-touch, and then both drop hands and turn away (man to right and lady to left) with four steps in a complete turn.

### Part Two. (MUSIC B)

MEAS. 1—8 (Repeated). Facing again, partners take closed dance position and do sixteen two-steps moving counter-clockwise around the floor.

RECORD: Imperial 1094.

# Cotton-Eyed Joe

●●●●●●●●●●●●●●●●●●●●●●●●●●●●●●●●●●●● UNITED STATES

This Southwestern couple dance is done to an old fiddle tune, and was described in Texas in the early 1880's as "nothing but a heel and toe 'poker.' " The description given here uses a two-step as the basic action; it may also be done with a polka throughout.

*Formation:* Couples in a double circle, men with backs to center. Lady does opposite footwork throughout.

### Part One. (MUSIC A)

MEAS. 1—2. In closed dance position, man hops on right foot and touches left heel out to left side, as lady does counterpart. He hops again on right, and touches left toe to floor in front of right. He does a two-step, left-right-left, in line of direction.

MEAS. 3—4. This action is repeated with the other foot leading, in the reverse direction.

MEAS. 5—8. Each dancer turns away for a solo turn (man to left, lady to right) with three two-steps beginning with outside foot. Returning to face each other, they take three quick stamps in place.

### Part Two. (MUSIC B)

MEAS. 1—4. Facing each other but not taking hands (man's left and lady's right hand may be held up) take four "chug" or "push" steps (see page 31) to man's left and lady's right. Immediately do four "chug" steps in reverse direction, lifting other hands.

MEAS. 5—8. In closed dance position, take four two-steps, turning clockwise and moving in the line of direction.

NOTE: Many individual variations, such as clog or hopping steps may be introduced in Part Two; the entire dance is very lively and free.

RECORD: Imperial 1045B; Educational Dance Recordings FD-3

# Boston Two-Step

•••••••••••••••••••••••••••••••••••••• ENGLAND

This old English ballroom dance has a special charm, very much like the "Oxford Minuet," but livelier throughout.

*Formation:* Couples in a double circle, facing counter-clockwise in open position (inside hands joined, outside hands on waist or with lady's free hand holding skirt).

### Part One. (MUSIC A)

MEAS. 1—2. Beginning with outside foot, each dancer does a pas de bas (see page 31) away from his partner, and then toward his partner.

MEAS. 3—4. Leading with the outside foot, each dancer walks three steps forward in the line of direction. Keeping the weight on the outside foot (man's left, lady's right) each dancer turns toward his partner on the fourth count, and faces in the reverse line of direction, now joining man's left and lady's right hand.

MEAS. 5—8. Repeat action of Meas. 1—4, doing the pas de bas apart and together, walking three steps clockwise, and turning to face partners on the fourth count.

### Part Two. (MUSIC A)

MEAS. 1—4. With both hands joined, do a pas de bas to man's left and lady's right, then another in the reverse direction. Take two slow step-draws to man's left and lady's right.

MEAS. 5—8. In closed dance position, take four two-steps turning clockwise and traveling in line of direction around circle.

RECORD: Folk Dance MH-3001.

# Karapyet

•••••••••••••••••••••••••••••••••••••• RUSSIA

This dance and the one that follows, "Kohanochka," are both favorites of folk dancers everywhere. "Karapyet" is a slang word for one who comes from the Caucasus, and the tune was a popular old Russian drinking song. Vyts Beliajus comments that the steps show Armenian influence.

*Formation:* Double circle of couples, men with backs to center.

### Part One. (MUSIC A)

MEAS. 1. In closed dance position, but turning slightly to face in line of direction, touch the toe of the outside foot next to the inside foot, at same time rising on the ball of the inside foot.

MEAS. 2. Taking weight on full inside foot, cross the outside foot over in front of it, and touch the toe again to the floor, again rising on the ball of the inside foot.

MEAS. 3—4. Leading with the outside foot, take three walking steps in the line of direction (man's left-right-left, lady's opposite footwork). Turn on the fourth count to face clockwise, without changing arm position, and touch the man's right and lady's left foot lightly to floor.

MEAS. 5—8. Repeat action of Meas. 1—4, in reverse line of direction.

### Part Two. (MUSIC B)

MEAS. 1—2. With inside hands joined, in open position, take two polka steps forward in line of direction. Done Russian style, this is more of a LEAP-step-step, than a hop-step-close-step. As each dancer starts forward, with his outside foot, the joined hands swing forward, and the free hands swing backward and out, at chest level. On the second polka, the joined hands swing back, and the free hands are swung across the chest.

MEAS. 3—4. Each dancer turns away (man to left, lady to right) with two polka steps, turning completely and continuing to move in line of direction.

MEAS. 5—8. Action of Meas. 1—4 is repeated.

### Part Three. (MUSIC B)

MEAS. 1—2. With inside hands still joined, partners face and walk three steps in line of direction, beginning with the outside foot. Swing the inside foot lightly across in front. Free arm is held out at shoulder height.

MEAS. 3—4. Same action is done in reverse line of direction: walk-two-three-swing.

MEAS. 5—6. Facing again in line of direction, dancers do two forward polka steps as in Part Two, Meas. 1—2.

MEAS. 7—8. Quickly taking ballroom dance position, dancers do two closed polka steps, turning once clockwise and moving in the line of direction.

NOTE: There are several modifications of the dance, such as doing a heel-and-toe step at the very beginning, or turning away from partners with four walking steps in Part Two, which make it easier for beginning dancers.

RECORD: Folk Dancer MH-1058; Educational Dance Recordings FD-4.

# Kohanochka

•••••••••••••••••••••••••••••••••••••••• RUSSIA

This Russian ballroom dance is much like "Karapyet," and should be done smoothly, with feet gliding along close to the floor.

*Formation:* Double circle of couples in open position (inside hands joined, outside hands across chest, palm toward body), facing counter-clockwise.

### Part One. (MUSIC A)

MEAS. 1—4. As in Part Two of "Karapyet," dancers take two polka steps forward, leading with outside foot, and turn away with two polka steps.

MEAS. 5—8. Action of Meas. 1—4 is repeated.

### Part Two. (MUSIC B)

MEAS. 1—2. In Varsovienne position facing counter-clockwise, both man and lady balance forward on the left foot, and balance back on the right foot.

MEAS. 3—4. Beginning with the left foot, they take two Russian polka steps forward in line of direction.

MEAS. 5—8. Action of Meas. 1—4 is repeated.

### Part Three. (MUSIC C)

MEAS. 1—4. Partners face each other, men with backs to center of circle. They clap own hands twice. Man crosses arms in front of chest, as lady places hands on waist, and they move backward (apart) with three polka steps.

MEAS. 5—8. Again they clap twice and take three polka steps *forward*, passing partner's *left* side. The last polka may be emphasized by three stamps.

MEAS. 1—4. They clap twice again and take three polka steps *backward*, passing partner's *left* side.

MEAS. 5—6. They clap twice, pause, and shake right forefingers at each other.

MEAS. 7—8. Both turn away with two polka steps (man to left, lady to right) moving in line of direction. In some versions, partners strike right hands against each other, each turning to his own left, but this is considered to be unauthentic.

RECORD: Folk Dancer MH-1058; Educational Dance Recordings FD-4.

# Black Forest Mazurka

●●●●●●●●●●●●●●●●●●●●●●●●●●●●●● GERMANY

The mazurka step may be introduced in this lively little German dance.

*Formation:* Double circle of couples facing counter-clockwise in open position, with inside hands joined and free hands on waist.

### Part One

MEAS. 1—2. Starting with the outside foot, take two open waltz steps forward, balancing slightly apart and together as this is done.

MEAS. 3—4. Releasing hands and starting with the outside foot, the man turns away completely to his left, and lady to her right, with three walking steps. Facing each other, they clap their own hands three times.

### Part Two

MEAS. 5—6. They take ballroom dance position, but turn to face in the line of direction. Starting with the outside foot, they do two mazurka steps forward (see page 29). Men steps: left, right, hop on right (lifting left), and repeats this, as lady does opposite footwork.

MEAS. 7—8. Still in ballroom dance position, both turn with six walking steps, lady stepping forward toward center to begin the turn, and man backing up away from the center (counter-clockwise turn).

NOTE: While the steps are simple, the music is very fast and should be slowed down when the dance is first taught.

RECORD: Folk Dancer MH-1048.

# Varsovienne

Versions of this dance are found in many countries and authorities argue about its source. Some are certain that it was first done in Poland and named after the city of Warsaw. Others state that it was Italian, named after Mt. Vesuvius. One prominent expert calls it French, but most agree that it is really Swedish. All this demonstrates the difficulty of establishing dance genealogy!

*Diagram* 29

*Formation:* Couples in a double circle, facing counter-clockwise in Varsovienne position (Diagram 29) (*this* is the dance the position was named after!).

### Part One. (MUSIC A)

MEAS. 1—2. Beginning with the left foot, the man crosses behind his partner in three steps, traveling to the right, as she takes three steps, crossing in front of him. She is now on his left. Both place right heel diagonally forward and to the right side, toes pointing up, and hold. The hand position remains unchanged (Diagram 29).

MEAS. 3—4. The same action is done in reverse: beginning with the right foot, both partners cross over in three steps and point left heel diagonally forward on floor. Hold one count.

MEAS. 5—8. The action of Meas. 1—4 is repeated.

### Part Two. (MUSIC B)

MEAS. 1—4. Leading with the left foot, both dancers take two mazurka steps forward, and then cross over and point right heels, as in Meas. 1—2, Part One.

MEAS. 5—8. Leading with the right foot, both dancers take two mazurka steps forward and then cross over and point left heels, as in Meas. 3—4, Part One.

### Part Three. (MUSIC C)

MEAS. 1—8. In closed dance position, each couple waltzes counter-clockwise around the floor eight waltz steps.

NOTE: In another form of this dance, sometimes done by Swedes in the United States, a "conversation position" is used, and the lady crosses over and back in front of the man as he dances in place, during the first part of the dance.

RECORD: Folk Dancer MH-1023; Educational Dance Recordings FD-4.

# Eide Ratas

This traditional Estonian dance (the name means "spinning wheel") makes use of a vigorous form of the mazurka step.

*Formation:* Couples in a double circle facing counter-clockwise in semi-closed position.

### Part One. (MUSIC A)

MEAS. 1—2. Beginning with the outside foot, each couple does a mazurka step forward, in the line of direction. The first step forward is taken as a *leap*, with the body leaning forward. As the dancer comes sharply forward with the inside foot on the second step, and hops on the third, the body is straightened. The mazurka step is repeated.

MEAS. 3—4. Keeping semi-closed position, each couple turns in place with six steps, man stepping forward (away from center) and lady stepping backward.

MEAS. 5—8 and 1—8 (Repeated). The action of Meas. 1—4 is repeated three more times.

### Part Two. (MUSIC B)

MEAS. 1—2. Partners face each other (men with backs to center), placing hands on own waist. Beginning with the left foot, they take one waltz step backward, turning slightly to the left, and then another waltz step backward with the right foot leading, turning slightly to the right.

MEAS. 3—4. The action of Meas. 1—2 is repeated.

MEAS. 5—6. Partners clap own hands and run forward with six running steps, toward each other.

MEAS. 7—8. Linking right elbows they turn in place with six running steps, moving clockwise. Men end on the outside and ladies on the inside of the circle.

MEAS. 1—8 (Repeated). Repeat action of Meas. 1—8: four waltz steps backward, clap, six running steps forward, hook *left* elbows, turn once-and-a-half counter-clockwise with six steps, and end in original positions, to begin the dance again.

RECORD: Folk Dancer MH-1018A; Educational Dance Recordings FD-3.

# *Varsouvianna*

●●●●●●●●●●●●●●●●●●●●●●●●●●●●● UNITED STATES AND MEXICO

This dance is known throughout the American Southwest as "Put Your Little Foot." Supposedly it was learned from Polish nobility in the Mexican court of Maximilian, and then crossed the border.

*Formation*: Couples in a double circle, facing counter-clockwise, in Varsovienne position.

*Part One.* (MUSIC A) This is like Part Two of the Swedish Varsouvienne.

MEAS. 1. Both dancers step diagonally forward with the left foot with a long gliding step, take a closing step with the right foot, and hold the weight on the right foot, sweeping the left foot across in front of the right.

MEAS. 2. This action is repeated, with the left foot leading again.

MEAS. 3—4. As the man steps left-right-left, almost in place, the lady crosses over in front of him, left-right-left. Both point right feet diagonally forward to the right.

MEAS. 5—8. Action of Meas. 1—4 is repeated in reverse, with the right foot leading: step right, left (sweep right); step right, left (sweep right); right, left, right, point left, with cross-over.

*Part Two.* (MUSIC B)

MEAS. 1—2. The "crossover" action of Meas. 3—4, Part One, is repeated as a "short phrase," with the lady crossing left in front of the man, and both pointing right.

MEAS. 3—4. She crosses back in front of him, as in Meas. 7—8, Part One., and both point left.

MEAS. 5—8. Action of Meas. 1—4 is repeated.

NOTE: There are many other regional variations of the dance, including some in which the lady twirls out under the man's hand and back, and others in which there is a waltz sequence, as in the original Varsovienne.

RECORD: Folk Dancer MH-3016; Windsor 7615-B.

# Masquerade

•••••••••••••••••••••••••••••••••••••••••  DENMARK

This dance is interesting because of its variety of actions and rhythms.

**Formation:** Double circle of couples facing counter-clockwise.

### Part One. (MUSIC A)

MEAS. 1—4. Partners link inside arms (lady's left resting on man's right forearm) and walk sixteen steps forward.

MEAS. 5—8. They turn toward each other to face in the reverse direction (clockwise), link inside arms and walk sixteen steps in this direction.

### Part Two. (MUSIC B)

MEAS.1—4. Turning to face counter-clockwise again, partners join inside hands and do four open waltzes forward, beginning with the outside foot: apart and together, apart and together.

MEAS. 5—8. In closed dance position they do four waltz steps, turning twice clockwise, and traveling counter-clockwise around the circle.

MEAS. 1—8. (Repeated). Repeat action of Meas. 1—8.

### Part Three. (MUSIC C)

MEAS. 1—4. With inside hands joined and facing counter-clockwise, each couple does four step-hop-swings (apart and together, apart and together), starting with the outside foot and moving forward around the circle. As they step on the outside foot, hop on it, and swing the inside foot across, the joined hands are swung forward. When they step on the inside foot, hop on it and swing the outside foot across, the joined hands are swung back.

MEAS. 5—8. Taking shoulder-waist position and beginning with the man's left foot and lady's right, each couple does four step-hops, turning twice clockwise and moving counter-clockwise around the circle.

MEAS. 1—8 (Repeated). Repeat action of Meas. 1—8.

RECORD: Folk Dancer MH-1019; Educational Dance Recordings FD-2.

# La Danza

In this old Italian dance—so the story goes—peasants used to imitate the nobility doing their elaborate, courtly dances. The steps should therefore be done with extravagant gestures and flourishes, except for the final part, which is a vigorous and peasant-like step-hop, needing no exaggeration.

**Formation:** Double circle of couples facing counter-clockwise, in promenade position. Right hands are joined *under* left hands (both crossed in front).

### Part One. (MUSIC A)

MEAS. 1. Both step forward with the right foot, then step forward with the left foot with a closing step, taking the weight. Again step forward with the right and close with the left.

MEAS. 2. Step forward with the right foot, hold one count, and lightly touch the left toe forward in front of the right, not taking the weight. Hold.

MEAS. 3—4. Repeat this action with the left foot leading: left-together, left-together, left, touch right.

MEAS. 5—8. Step backward on the right foot and lightly touch the left toe forward. Step backward on the left, and touch the right toe forward. Repeat this action: back right, touch left, back left, touch right.

MEAS. 1—8. (Repeated). Repeat action of Meas. 1—8.

### Part Two. (MUSIC B)

MEAS. 1—2. Partners face. Under raised, joined hands, lady does a left face turn in three steps. Both do a deep bow or curtsey, releasing hands.

MEAS. 3—4. Resuming crossed-hand position, partners change places in three steps: man walks straight over and does half right-face turn to face partner; lady does left-face turn under joined hands as she crosses over. Both bow or curtsey.

MEAS. 5—6. Both join right hands only and cross over to change places, with lady making a left-face turn under joined hands. Both bow or curtsey.

MEAS. 7—8. Both join left hands and cross over, lady doing a right-face turn under joined hands. Both bow or curtsey.

MEAS. 1—4 (Repeated). Both hook right elbows, change places and bow or curtsey. Both hook left elbows, change places, and bow or curtsey.

MEAS. 5—8 (Repeated). Partners take shoulder-waist position and do eight step-hops, turning clockwise and moving counter-clockwise around the circle.

RECORD: Folk Dancer MH-1045

# *Corrido*

This dance is a combination of several traditional Mexican dance steps, as performed to the type of folk ballad known as a "corrido." The version described here was learned by the California Folk Dance Federation from a teacher who had observed it in Mexico.

**Formation:** Double circle of couples, partners facing, men with backs to center of circle. Closed dance position.

### *Part One.* (MUSIC A)

MEAS. 1—5. Beginning with the man's right and lady's left, take ten short step-draws, moving clockwise around the circle. The movement is to the side and has a characteristic body sway, like the rumba.

### *Part Two.* (MUSIC B)

MEAS. 1—8. Starting with the man's right and lady's left foot crossing in front, take seven grapevine steps moving counter-clockwise around the circle. Then the man crosses with the right foot, stamps with the left and stamps right in place, as the lady does opposite footwork.

### *Part Three.* (MUSIC C)

MEAS. 1—2. Starting with the man's right and lady's left, take *four* short step-draws moving clockwise around the circle.

MEAS. 3—10. "*Soldado.*" Beginning with the man's right and lady's left, take four shuffling steps (man backing up, lady going forward) diagonally toward the center of the floor and veering slightly toward the man's left. Then, turning the body slightly so right sides become adjacent, the couple takes four shuffling steps diagonally *away* from the center of the circle and to the man's left. Repeat this entire action three times more, moving toward and away from the center and traveling counter-clockwise around the circle. On the final "soldado," moving away from the center, the man steps right, stamps left and right, and holds, as the lady does the opposite.

**Part Four.** (MUSIC B)

MEAS. 1—8. Repeat the grapevine as in Part Two.

NOTE: This is the basic sequence of the dance. When it is repeated a *second time*, the following steps replace the grapevine sequences.

**First Grapevine Variation** (for Part Two): (MUSIC B)

MEAS. 1. Partners face, man with hands behind back, lady holding skirt out to side. Man begins by stepping with his right foot across in front of his left, stepping with the left in place, stepping with right in place, and crossing the left foot in front of right, lifting right foot from floor.

MEAS. 2. Man does a full left-face turn in place, starting by crossing his right foot behind the left, and pivoting with three more steps, left, right, left, to face his partner. (Throughout Meas. 1—2) lady does opposite footwork.

MEAS. 3—8. The action of Meas. 1—2 is done three times more. On the last measure, instead of turning left, the man crosses right foot in front, stamps left, stamps right, and holds, as lady does opposite footwork.

**Second Grapevine Variation** (for Part Four): (MUSIC B)

MEAS. 1—8. Partners join right hands at shoulder height, with man's free hand behind back and lady's hand holding skirt. Starting with right foot, man does seven grapevine steps. Meanwhile lady, starting with left foot, does the grapevine (crossing in front and behind) and then twirls rapidly with a right-face turn *twice*, under the man's hand, moving in the line of direction. She repeats this entire action twice more, and does one more grapevine. On the final measure, the man crosses his right foot over in front of left, stamps with left, stamps with right, and holds, as lady does opposite footwork.

NOTE: The dance is repeated a third time, just as it was done the first time, except that on the final grapevine sequence (Part Four) partners hold inside hands, accent the movement apart and together, throw free hand up in the air and let out a little yell on the last note of music.

RECORD: "Eso Si, Eso No," Columbia 6196X.

# Neapolitan Tarantella

•••••••••••••••••••••••••••••••••••••••••• ITALY

There are probably hundreds of different tarantella steps and sequences. The version of the tarantella described here has been popular with folk dance groups, both on the East and West Coast of the United States.

*Formation:* Couples in a double circle, partners facing, men with backs to center. Lady should have a tambourine in her left hand.

### Part One. (MUSIC A)

MEAS. 1. Both man and lady do a pas de bas (see page 31) to their own right, raising the right arm overhead and bringing the left arm over in front of the chest.

MEAS. 2. Do the pas de bas to the left, reversing the arm position.

MEAS. 3—4. Action of Meas. 1—2 is repeated.

MEAS. 5—8. Partners place right arms around each other's waist and, with left hand high, do four step-hops starting with the right foot, turning once clockwise.

MEAS. 1—8. (Repeated). Repeat action of Meas. 1—8.

### Part Two. (MUSIC B)

MEAS. 1—4. Partners face counter-clockwise and join inside hands. Man takes eight steps in place as lady takes eight running steps, moving in front of him and coming around behind him to place, passing joined hands over his head.

MEAS. 5—6. With inside hands still joined, partners do a pas de bas apart and together.

MEAS. 7—8. They drop hands and as the man claps and the lady strikes the tambourine on the first count, they make a complete turn in four steps (man to left, lady to right) away from each other and back to the starting position.

MEAS. 1—8 (Repeated). Repeat action of Meas. 1—8.

### Part Three. (MUSIC A)

MEAS. 1—2. Bending forward with arms stretched out in back, partners take four walking steps forward, toward each other. They straighten up, bring arms forward, and on the fourth count strike the tambourine or clap sharply overhead.

MEAS. 3—4. Repeat this action in reverse, backing away, and striking the tambourine behind the back on the fourth count.

MEAS. 5—8. Shaking tambourine or snapping fingers overhead, partners go forward and "do-si-do" in eight steps, passing right shoulders, moving back to back, and backing up to place, passing left shoulders.

MEAS. 1—8 (Repeated). The action of Meas. 1—8 is repeated, except that the second "do-si-do" is done with the left shoulder leading.

*Part Four.* (MUSIC B)

MEAS. 1—6. In closed dance position, couples do six polka steps around the floor.

MEAS. 7—8. Lady twirls twice with a right-face turn, under the man's left hand, holding her right.

MEAS. 1—8 (Repeated) Action of Meas. 1—8 is repeated.

RECORD: Harmonia H2051A (note irregular introduction of five measures); Elektra EKL-206.

# Attached Couple Dances

.............................................. *9*

*THIS CHAPTER CONTAINS* a variety of "attached" couple dances. These are dances which, unlike those in the preceding chapter, are done in the circle formation, in two couple sets, or with couples progressing to meet other couples traveling around the floor in the opposite direction.

A number of them are based on steps that are very similar to those found in the couple dances described earlier. Others, particularly the English and American dances, are based on actions like the "ladies chain," "right and left through," "arming," and "siding," which are not so much dance steps as they are patterns of movement about the floor. Again, they are presented in approximate order of difficulty.

# *Sudmalinas*

**......................................** L A T V I A

The name of this dance means the "little mill." It is based on the polka and waltz and is a spirited mixer which moves rapidly, but is not difficult.

*Formation:* Sets of two couples facing each other, scattered around the floor (Diagram 8). Each lady is on her partner's right.

### *Part One.* (MUSIC A)

MEAS. 1—8. All four join hands in a circle and starting with the right foot, do six polka steps to the right. Each person claps his own hands three times.
MEAS. 1—8 (Repeated). Action of Meas. 1—8 is repeated to the left.

### *Part Two.* (MUSIC B)

MEAS. 1—8 (music is repeated). In shoulder–waist position, each couple does sixteen polka steps around the other couple, turning clockwise and moving counter-clockwise around them.

### *Part Three.* (MUSIC C)

MEAS. 1—8. In the starting formation, four dancers join right hands in a right hand star, holding the hands high. They take six polka steps to the left (clockwise) and clap their own hands three times.
MEAS. 1—8 (Repeated). Action of Meas. 1—8 is repeated with a left hand star, traveling to the right.

### *Part Four.* (MUSIC D)

MEAS. 1—8. Each man takes the opposite lady as his partner. With her, he does four open waltz steps and four closed turning waltzes, as in Part Two of Masquerade (Page 110).
MEAS. 1—8 (Repeated). Action of Meas. 1—8 is repeated.

NOTE: At the end of the waltz section, each couple finds a new couple to begin the dance with again.

RECORD: RCA Victor LPM 1621.

# Little Man in a Fix

Since each couple must find a new couple to dance with, when the dance is repeated, the man of the couple is "in a fix"—if he cannot locate them! Although this dance is Danish, similar actions are found in other Scandinavian dances.

*Formation:* Sets of two couples, scattered around the floor. Each man has his right arm around his partner, and hooks left elbows with the opposite man. (Diagram 30)

### Part One. (MUSIC A)

MEAS. 1—8. Beginning with the left foot, take twenty-four running steps forward (eight running waltzes) lightly accenting the first step of each waltz. Ladies lean slightly forward.

MEAS. 1—8 (Repeated). Men draw apart slightly, join left hands with each other, and hold their partner's left hands in their right. The ladies move forward, pass in front of their partners, turn left, go under the arch formed by the men's joined left hands. They continue to turn left (Diagram 31) and join right hands with each other over the man's joined left hands. The entire group moves with running steps in the counter-clockwise direction throughout this, and when hands are joined in the final position they continue to run.

### Part Two. (MUSIC B)

MEAS. 1—4. Each man holds his partner's left hand in his right; all other hands are released. Couples stand back to back with each other and, traveling away from each other, do four open waltz steps, balancing apart and together twice.

MEAS. 5—8. Each couple does four closed, turning waltzes, moving freely around the floor.

MEAS. 1—8 (Repeated). Action of Meas. 1—8 is repeated.

NOTE: Each couple immediately finds a new couple with which to repeat the dance. In one version of the dance, men without partners may "cut in" during the closed waltz section of Part Two. The person who is "cut out" immediately tries to get another partner. Whoever is left without a partner when the dance begins again becomes the "Little Man in a Fix."

RECORD: Folk Dancer MH-1054; Educational Dance Recordings FD-4.

(top)   Diagram 30

(above)   Diagram 31

# Sicilian Tarantella

•••••••••••••••••••••••••••••••••••••••••• ITALY

This version of the popular Tarantella is based on a number of typical Sicilian steps, and is done, like the preceding two dances, in sets of two couples.

*Formation:* Two-couple sets, men standing side by side with each other, facing their partners. As in a Virginia Reel, the "head" couple is nearest the music; the "foot" couple is farthest from the music.

### Part One. (MUSIC A)

MEAS. 1—4. In place and facing partner, each person steps on his right foot, hops on it, swinging the left foot forward, and at the same time claps his own hands (or strikes a tambourine). This is repeated doing the step-hop on the left foot and swinging the right foot forward and clapping. In place, take four quick running steps, snapping fingers or shaking a tambourine overhead.

MEAS. 5—8 (and 1—8, repeated). Repeat above, three times more.

### Part Two. (MUSIC B)

MEAS. 1—8 (music is repeated). Snapping fingers or shaking tambourines, each dancer bends forward, runs four steps toward his partner, straightening up and raising his arms. He takes four steps backward, lowering arms and bending forward. This is done three times more.

### Part Three. (MUSIC C)

MEAS. 1—8 (music is repeated). The "head" man and "foot" lady (diagonally opposite, see Diagram 32) clap own hands, run forward, hook right elbows, turn once and return to place taking an extra right-face twirl as they come back. The "foot" man and "head" lady do the same thing. The same action is repeated with a *left*-elbow turn, first with the "head" man and "foot" lady, and then other couple.

MUSIC A

MEAS. 1—8 (music is repeated). The "head" man and "foot" lady do a right shoulder do-si-do and return to place. The other couple does the same. The "head" man and "foot" lady do a left shoulder do-si-do, and then the other couple does the same.

*Diagram 32*

**Part Four.** (MUSIC B)

MEAS. 1—8. Each person faces to his own right and with hands on waists, all skip forward (counter-clockwise) for eight steps in the circle. Turning about, they skip in the reverse direction (clockwise) for eight steps.

MEAS. 1—8 (Repeated). All four dancers join left hands in a star and skip counter-clockwise for eight steps. They turn, make a right-hand star, and skip clockwise for eight steps. They return to their regular position to begin the dance again.

RECORD: RCA Victor LPM 1621; Educational Dance Recordings FD-4.

# Sellenger's Round

................................................ ENGLAND

One of the oldest and best known English country dances, this is said to have been danced in Queen Elizabeth's day. It is a good dance for May Day celebrations, and also as a lead-up to teaching "Black Nag."

*Formation:* Couples in a single circle with hands joined, facing center. Each lady on partner's right.

### Part One. (MUSIC A)

MEAS. 1—8. All take eight sliding (slipping) steps to left, and then to right.

### Chorus. (MUSIC B)

MEAS. 1—2. All do two balance (setting) steps to center. Leap diagonally forward and to right with right foot, and take two quick steps (left, right) in place. Repeat action, leaping forward with left foot, and two quick steps (right, left) in place.

MEAS. 3—4. All take four walking steps backward (a double), moving away from center.

MEAS. 5—6. Release hands and all face partners, with arms at sides. Balance (set) sideways, to the right, and to the left.

MEAS. 7—8. All turn single, turning individually with right-face turn in four steps.

MEAS. 1—8 (Repeated). Repeat action of Meas. 1—8.

### Part Two. (MUSIC A)

MEAS. 1—8. With hands joined in the circle, all take four walking steps (forward a double) into the center, and four walking steps back. This is repeated. Then do entire CHORUS.

### Part Three. (MUSIC A)

MEAS. 1—8. "Siding." Partners face each other and walk forward with four steps, passing left shoulders and turning left to face each other again on the fourth step. They walk back to place, passing right shoulders, and turn right to face each other on the fourth step. This action is repeated. Then do entire CHORUS.

### Part Four. (MUSIC A)

MEAS. 1—8. "Arming." Partners face each other, hook right elbows and turn clockwise with eight light running steps. They then hook left elbows and turn counter-clockwise. Then do entire CHORUS.

**Part Five.** (MUSIC A)

MEAS. 1—8. All slide eight steps to left and right, as in Part One. Then do entire CHORUS.

RECORD: RCA Victor LPM 1621; Folkraft 1174-B; Educational Dance Recordings FD-3.

## Circle Hopak

**···································· AMERICAN-UKRAINIAN**

The couple Hopak is a spectacular and difficult dance—far beyond the ability of the ordinary dancer. The circle dance described here was learned by the author in New York's Play Co-op, and is a simple but enjoyable routine set to the music of the Hopak.

*Formation:* Single circle of couples with hands joined, facing center. Lady on her partner's right.

MUSIC A

MEAS. 1—4. Holding hands in circle, all stamp strongly with right foot eight times, pausing after each stamp. Take weight on the right foot on the last stamp.

MUSIC B

MEAS. 1—4. With hands still joined, all leap to the left and with the left foot, and cross right foot behind it, taking the weight. This action is done eight times, traveling to the left in the circle.

MUSIC A

MEAS. 1—4. All face partners and place right arms around partner's waist, with left hand raised above shoulder, elbow bent. All swing with eight Czardas swing steps. This is somewhat like a slow buzz swing, but with more of a down-up effect: dip *down* stepping on the right foot and come *up* on the left foot. Partners lean away from each other during this.

MUSIC B

MEAS. 1—4. Releasing partners, all face center. They run forward, into center, four steps, clapping own hands in front on the fourth step. They run backward (away from center) four steps and clap hands behind backs on fourth step. This action is repeated.

RECORD: Kismet A-106; Methodist World of Fun M-110.

# *Waltz Country Dance*

..................................................... ENGLAND

This progressive circle dance is a favorite at festivals of the Country Dance Society, where it is taught by May Gadd.

*Formation:* Double circle of couples facing couples (Diagram 7).

### *Part One.* (MUSIC A)

MEAS. 1—4. Each man joins right hands with the opposite lady. With the right foot leading, they balance forward and back (with a waltz balance) and then cross over, changing places with two waltz steps. The lady does a left-face turn during the crossover.

MEAS. 5—8. Each man faces his original partner, joins right hands with her, and repeats the action of Meas. 1—4, balancing forward and back, and crossing over.

MEAS. 1—8. (Repeated). Action of Meas. 1—8 is repeated, first with opposite and then with partner. Couples are now back in their original position.

### *Part Two.* (MUSIC B)

MEAS. 1—4. Join hands in a circle of four. All balance forward and back (man with left foot, lady with right). Each man drops his partner's hand but holds the hand of his left-hand lady, bringing her across in front of him with two waltz steps (making a right-face turn) to stand at his right side.

MEAS. 5—8. Again join hands, balance forward and back, and pass left-hand lady on to man's right.

MEAS. 1—8 (Repeated). Repeat action of Meas. 1—8, twice more.

### *Part Three.* (MUSIC C)

MEAS. 1—8. Each couple takes closed position; they waltz forward and to the right, and with eight waltz steps travel completely around the opposite couple (counter-clockwise) and move on to face a new couple. They begin the dance again with them.

RECORD: Folkraft 3363.

# Spanish Circle Waltz

This graceful, flowing dance, dating back to the mid-Nineteenth Century, is quite similar to the English Waltz Country Dance.

*Formation:* Double circle of couples facing couples (Diagram 7).

### Part One. (MUSIC A)

MEAS. 1—4. Couples take open position, inside hands joined, free hands on waist, or with lady's hand holding skirt. Leading with the outside foot, they waltz balance forward and back, toward the opposite couple. Release partner's hand, join inside hands (man's right, lady's left) with opposite person, and change places with two waltz steps, lady doing left-face turn under man's hand. Each person has now moved one-quarter of the way around the small circle (man going clockwise, lady counter-clockwise).

MEAS. 5—8. Action of Meas. 1—4 is repeated, with each man holding inside hands with lady now on his right, balancing forward and back to the opposite couple, joining inside hands with lady he is facing (his original partner) and changing places with her.

MEAS. 1—8 (Repeated). Action of Meas. 1—8 is repeated. Each couple is now back in original position.

### Part Two. (MUSIC B)

MEAS. 1—8. Each couple joins right hands in a star with the opposite couple and does four forward waltz steps, traveling clockwise, with them. They turn, make a left-hand star and do four waltz steps, moving counter-clockwise and back to original position.

### Part Three

MEAS. 1—8 (Repeated). As in Part Three of Waltz County Dance, each couple, in closed position, does eight turning waltz steps, traveling counter-clockwise around the opposite couple, and progressing on to face a new couple to begin the dance with again.

RECORD: RCA Victor LPM 1620; Folkraft 1047; Educational Dance Recordings FD-4.

## Portland Fancy

This is a traditional circle progressive dance, similar to contra, or "line" dances. Many of the actions in it are also found in American square dances.

*Formation:* Lines of two couples facing two couples, like spokes of a wheel, radiating from the center (Diagram 33).

*Diagram 33*

### Part One. (MUSIC A)

MEAS. 1—8. Joining hands in the lines of four, and linking the lines at the ends to make a circle of eight, all walk sixteen steps to the left (clockwise), ending in original positions.

### Part Two. (MUSIC B)

MEAS. 1—4. *Right and left through.* Each couple passes through the couple directly opposite it (Diagram 34), with the lady passing *between* the opposite couple, and man passing on the outside (another way to explain it is to have each person pass *right* shoulders with the person he is facing). This is done in four steps. Each man joins left hands with his partner and places his right hand over her right hand, at her waist, and they do a *courtesy turn*, pivoting counter-clockwise as a couple in four steps. (Diagram 35).

MEAS. 5—8. Each couple does a *right and left through* with the same opposite couple, returning to place and doing the *courtesy turn* to face in original direction.

### Part Three. (MUSIC C)

MEAS. 1—4. *Ladies Chain.* The lady in each couple walks forward, joins right hands with the opposite lady and passes her. She gives left hand to the left hand of the opposite man, and he turns her with a *courtesy turn.*

MEAS. 5—8. *The ladies chain* is repeated, back to original position.

### Part Four. (MUSIC A)

MEAS. 1—4. Joining hands in lines of four, each line walks forward four steps, and backward four steps.

MEAS. 5—8. Again they advance four steps, and dropping hands, pass through the opposite line, and progress to meet a new line of four. They will begin the dance again with them.

RECORD: World of Fun M-104; Folkraft 1131-A; Educational Dance Recordings FD-3.

*(above)* **Diagram 34**
*(right)* **Diagram 35**

## Fireman's Dance

•••••••••••••••••••••••••••••••••••••••••••••• UNITED STATES

This rollicking dance is an early American favorite, and supposedly was featured at every "Fireman's Ball."

*Formation:* Lines of two couples facing two couples, as in Portland Fancy (Diagram 33). The couples closest to the center are Number One Couples; those on the outside are Number Two Couples.

### Part One. (MUSIC A)

MEAS. 1—4. Both the Number One man and the opposite Number One lady who are nearest the center (at the end of the line) step forward and join both hands. At the same time, the Number Two man and opposite Number Two lady at the other end of the line take one step back. The active Number Ones, with hands joined, slide eight steps down the center, between the lines (Diagram 36), while the active Number Twos take eight slides (individually) behind their lines.

Diagram 36

MEAS. 5—8. They return to place with eight slides, Ones still on the inside and Twos on the outside.

MEAS. 1—8 (Repeated). The reverse of Meas. 1—8 is done, with the end Twos joining hands and sliding down center and back, *between* the lines, and the end Ones stepping back and sliding *behind* the lines and back to place.

### Part Two. (MUSIC B)

MEAS. 1—8. Simultaneously, the Number One couples do a *right and left through*, over and back to place, while the Number Twos do a *ladies chain*, over and back (see Portland Fancy, page 126).

MEAS. 1—8 (Repeated). Simultaneously, the Number One couples do a *ladies chain* over and back, while the Number Twos do a *right and left through*, over and back.

### Part Three. (MUSIC C)

MEAS. 1—8. As in Part Four of Portland Fancy, with hands joined in lines of four, all advance four steps, shouting "Fire! Fire! Fire! Fire!" and walk backward four steps, shouting "Water! Water! Water! Water!" They then release hands, walk forward, and pass through the opposite line, progressing to begin the dance with a new opposite line.

NOTE: The *right and left through* and *ladies chain* should be practiced in another dance (such as Portland Fancy) before doing Fireman's Dance, so these basic actions are thoroughly familiar. Otherwise Part Two may be too confusing. Some directions and record calls refer to the couples as "Here" and "There," but the action is the same.

RECORD: World of Fun M-107; Folkraft 1131-B; Educational Dance Recordings FD-4.

# Kreuz Koenig

•••••••••••••••••••••••••••••••••••••••••  GERMANY

A difficult dance which makes a fine exhibition number, "Kreuz Koenig" has been translated both as "King's Cross" and "King of Clubs." Either term describes the shape of some of the dance's actions . . .

*Formation:* Sets of two couples facing, scattered around the floor. Each lady is on her partner's right.

### Part One. (MUSIC A)

MEAS. 1—2. With hands joined in a circle of four, all leap out to the left with the left foot, cross the right foot behind the left, taking the weight, and, turning slightly to the left, take four running steps: left, right, left, right. Leaning back during this action adds momentum.

MEAS. 3—8. Repeat action of Meas. 1—2, three times more.

### Part Two. (MUSIC A)

MEAS. 1—8. Men hook left elbows with each other, and place right arms around partner's waist. Lady's left hand is extended behind partner's back, and grips other man's left hand. All run forward (counter-clockwise) eight running waltzes, as in the Danish Little Man in a Fix, beginning with left foot.

### Part Three. (MUSIC B)

MEAS. 1—4. Releasing hands, couples face each other. As ladies step-hop twice in place, men pass each other with two step-hops (starting left), and momentarily taking each other's left hand. They join right hands with the opposite lady and turn clockwise with two step-hops.

MEAS. 5—8. Men join left hands and pass each other, returning to partner's left side with two step-hops. They join right hands with partners, and ladies do right-face turn under joined hands and then curtsey, as men bow.

MEAS. 1—8 (Repeated). Repeat action of Meas. 1—8.

### Part Four. (MUSIC C)

MEAS. 1—4. Join hands in circle of four, and, beginning left and moving clockwise, take four mazurka steps.

MEAS. 5—8. Men face their own partners, join hands and, beginning left and turning clockwise, take two mazurka steps. They then do six running steps, still turning clockwise. On the last step, the man's left hand releases the lady's right and they open up to rejoin the circle of four with the other couple.

*Diagram* 37

MEAS. 1—8 (Repeated). Repeat action of Meas. 17—24, but at end, during the six running steps, men take their partner's right hand in their right and move the ladies so they are in the center, back to back (Diagram 37).

*Part Five.* (MUSIC D)

MEAS. 1—4. Holding partner's right hand in their right, men take the opposite lady's left hand in their left, and, pulling slightly away (so the lady's arms are taut) take twelve running steps to the left. Ladies take running steps pivoting in place.

MEAS. 5—8. Holding partner's right hand, but dropping other lady's left, men slide into the center (left shoulder leading) so they are back to back, as ladies move out to "end" position. This quick change of position is marked by a stamp on the first step. Ladies run twelve steps to the left, as men revolve in center.

MEAS. 1—8 (Repeated). Repeat action of Meas. 1—8, with men swinging out again (as ladies move to the center) and then ladies swinging out (as men move to the center). *Always* hold partner's right hand through this sequence.

NOTE: When the dance has been completed, and all turn in place to face the center, each man has the opposite lady on his right. The dance may then be repeated, with this new partner, from the beginning.

RECORD: Folk Dancer MH-1022.

## Fado Blanquita

This dance is described by different authorities as being Spanish, Portuguese, and Portuguese-Brazilian. Of the many versions done by folk dance groups in the United States, this is one of the most appealing.

*Formation:* Couples with hands joined in a single circle, facing center, lady on partner's right.

### Part One

MEAS. 1—4. Starting with left foot, all circle left with sixteen light running steps.

MEAS. 5—8. All circle right with sixteen running steps.

### Part Two. (MUSIC B)

MEAS. 1—2. All face partners, join right hands (elbows bent, fingers pointing up), and sway to right, left, right, and left. Weight briefly shifts to right foot, left, right, and left, during this two-measure interlude.

MEAS. 3—5. With right hands joined and free hand on waist, partners do three schottische steps around each other, starting with the right foot and keeping the step smooth: right-left-right-hop, left-right-left-hop, right-left-right-hop. The steps are short, and should bring each dancer just far enough around to face his corner.

MEAS. 6—8. Joining left hands with corners, each dancer does three schottisches around corner, starting with left foot, and returning to face partner.

MEAS. 9—14. Action of Meas. 3—8 is repeated.

MEAS. 15—16. To conclude Part Two, all face center, join hands, and sway to right (stepping lightly on right foot), to left (stepping on left), and three light stamps in place: right-left-right.

### Part Three. (MUSIC C)

MEAS. 1. With hands joined all jump in place on both feet, then hop on right foot, swinging left foot across in front. Again jump in place on both feet, hop on left, and swing right foot across in front.

MEAS. 2. Jump in place on both feet, and then jump, turning halfway round with a right-face turn, so each dancer is standing with back to center.

MEAS. 3—4. Join hands and repeat action of Meas. 1—2, ending facing center.

MEAS. 5—8. Slowly raising joined hands, walk four slow steps to center. Then, lowering hands, walk backward four slow steps, away from center.

MEAS. 1—8 (Repeated). Repeat action of Meas. 1—8.

RECORD: RCA Victor LPM 1620; Folkraft 1173; Educational Dance Recordings FD-4.

# Partner-Changing Dances

.................................... *10*

THE DANCES IN this chapter are fairly simple couple mixers which are based, for the most part, on familiar folk dance steps like the waltz, schottische, or two-step.

They are particularly useful when a class is learning to folk dance because, as students move from partner to partner, they practice the basic steps with each person they meet—and thus go through many quick, repeated "drills." They are also appropriate because of their simplicity and "fun" element, for recreational dance groups, or as a means of mixing up a group socially. Many of these dances are American and of comparatively recent origin.

# Oklahoma Mixer

In a slightly different form, this is known as the "Cowboy Schottische." Actually it is a typically relaxed Southwestern schottische mixer, in which the hop has been eliminated.

*Formation:* Double circle of couples facing counter-clockwise, lady on man's right, in Varsovienne position.

### Part One

MEAS. 1—2. Starting with the left foot, each person does a two-step diagonally forward and to the left, and then, starting with the right foot, a two-step diagonally forward to the left. The cue is: left-close-left (hold), right-close-right (hold).

MEAS. 3—4. Take four slow walking steps forward, with a slight strut, or swaggering effect.

### Part Two

MEAS. 5. Both man and lady place left heel diagonally forward and to the left (without having it take the weight) and then lightly touch left toe to the floor in front of right.

MEAS. 6. As they release right hands (still holding left) lady takes three steps (left-right-left, hold) crossing over in front of man and facing back (clockwise) toward the man behind her partner. Meanwhile, man takes three steps (left-right-left, hold) in place.

MEAS. 7. With the right foot, repeat heel-and-toe action of Meas. 5.

MEAS. 8. Lady takes three steps (right-left-right, hold) moving toward man behind her partner, and completing a left-face turn so she again faces counter-clockwise. Meanwhile, each man takes three steps diagonally forward and to the left (right-left-right, hold) to take this next lady as his partner, in Varsovienne position.

RECORD: Educational Dance Recordings FD-3, or any moderate tempo American schottische.

## Glowworm Mixer

••••••••••••••••••••••••••••••••••• UNITED STATES

The simplest of all couple mixers, this is based on a plain walking step.

*Formation:* Couples face counter-clockwise in a double circle, in promenade position. Footwork is the same for both partners.

MEAS. 1. Beginning with the left foot, walk four steps forward.

MEAS. 2. Releasing hands, partners face each other. Man backs up four steps toward center of circle, as lady backs up four steps, away from center.

MEAS. 3. Each person walks forward four steps, moving diagonally to the left, to meet a new partner.

MEAS. 4. Joining both hands with this partner (right crossed over left) each couple turns once clockwise, with four steps. They end facing counter-clockwise, to begin dance again from the beginning.

RECORD: Imperial 1044-A; MacGregor 310.

## Seven Steps (Siebenschritt)

••••••••••••••••••••••••••••••••••• GERMANY

A lively and enjoyable couple mixer which affords a good opportunity to practice the schottische.

*Formation:* Double circle of couples in open position (inside hands joined, free hands on waist) facing counter-clockwise.

### Part One. (MUSIC A)

MEAS. 1—2. Starting with the outside foot, run forward seven steps, pausing on the eighth count and lifting inside foot slightly, so toe touches floor.

MEAS. 3—4. Starting with inside foot, run backward seven steps, pausing on eighth count and lifting outside foot slightly.

### Part Two. (MUSIC B)

MEAS. 1—2. Releasing partner's hands, and with both hands on waist, each person does a schottische step to the side (man to left, lady to right), away from his partner. This may be three runs and a hop, or a side-close-side, hop. He does a schottische step returning to face his partner.

MEAS. 3—4. In shoulder-waist position, each couple turns once clockwise with four step-hops, starting with man's left and lady's right.

MEAS. 5—6. Again, partners do schottische step away from each other.

But, when they return with a schottische each man moves forward diagonally to *next* lady, and each lady moves back slightly to meet this new partner.

MEAS. 7—8. In shoulder-waist position, four step-hops with this partner.

RECORD: Folk Dancer MH-1048-A; Educational Dance Recordings FD-2.

# *Totur*

•••••••••••••••••••••••••••••••••••••• DENMARK

A favorite Danish couple mixer, based on the two-step or polka.

*Formation:* Single circle of couples facing center, with hands joined, each lady on her partner's right.

*Introduction:* Only done at the beginning of the dance (MUSIC A)

MEAS. 1—8. All take sixteen walking steps (or eight polka steps) to left, beginning with left foot.

MEAS. 1—8 (Repeated). Repeat action of Meas. 1—8 to right.

## *Part One.* (MUSIC B)

MEAS. 1—2. Taking semi-closed position (Diagram 14), each couple moves toward the center of the circle with one two-step and two walking steps. Man's action is: left-right-left, hold, walk right and left. Lady does opposite footwork.

MEAS. 3—4. Moving backward, away from center of circle, do same action in reverse. Man does: right-left-right, hold, walk left and right. Lady does opposite footwork.

MEAS. 5—8. Partners face, take closed dance position, and do four two-steps or polka steps, turning clockwise and moving in the line of direction around the circle.

MEAS. 1—8 (Repeated). Repeat action of Meas. 1—8.

## *Part Two.* (MUSIC C)

MEAS. 1—8. Partners face and do a grand right and left (man moving counter-clockwise and lady clockwise) around the circle, with sixteen walking or eight polka steps.

MEAS. 1—8 (Repeated). Continue grand right and left. At end, each person takes new partner and dance is repeated from Part One. If a dancer fails to find a partner immediately, he goes to the center of the circle to look for one.

RECORD: Folk Dancer MH-1021.

# Doudlebska Polka

...................................... CZECHOSLOVAKIA

The author learned this dance in 1956 at the College of the Pacific Folk Dance Camp in California, where it was one of the most popular new dances. It had been introduced earlier at Michael Herman's Folk Dance Camp by Jeanette Novak.

*Formation:* Couples scattered freely about the floor, in closed dance position.

*Part One.* (MUSIC A)

MEAS. 1—8. Couples do eight closed polka steps, turning clockwise and traveling counter-clockwise around the floor.

MEAS. 1—8 (Repeated). Repeat action of Meas. 1—8.

*Part Two.* (MUSIC B)

MEAS. 1—8. Couples form small circles (six or eight couples in a circle) and march briskly counter-clockwise, each man with his left hand on the left shoulder of the man in front of him, and his right arm around his partner's waist. They march sixteen steps.

MEAS. 1—8 (Repeated). They continue to march, sixteen additional steps.

*Part Three.* (MUSIC C)

MEAS. 1—8. Releasing partners, men form a single circle, facing center. As ladies polka individually, clockwise, around outside of circle, men clap their own hands twice and then clap hands once, with the men on either side of them. This action is done eight times.

MEAS. 1—8 (Repeated). Repeat action of Meas. 1—8. At end, men turn to face ladies and find a new partner to begin the dance with.

NOTE: Doudlebska Polka has many elements that make it a sure-fire hit: (1) Its music is lively and appealing, with the sections clearly marked; (2) It gives those without a partner a chance to cut in easily during the third part; (3) Dancers find it fun to sing the melody of the second part as they march around; (4) The action in which the men clap hands with each other has a mock-aggression aspect and they tend to "ham it up," as ladies polka daintily around the outside.

RECORD: Folk Dancer MH-3016; Educational Dance Recordings FD-2.

# *Napoleon*

**· · · · · · · · · · · · · · · · · · · · · · · · · · · · ·** DENMARK

This lively dance is of Danish origin, although words of an English chantey may be sung to it.

*Formation:* Double circle of couples, men with backs to center, facing partners. Hands grip partner's upper arms, as in Part One of Meitschi Putz Di.

### *Part One.* (MUSIC A)

MEAS. 1—2. Each man does a schottische to his left side, leading with the left foot, and then to his right, leading with the right, as the lady does opposite footwork.

MEAS. 3—4. Each person claps his own own hands once, claps right hands with his partner, claps his own hands, claps left hands with his partner, claps his own hands, and claps his partner's hands twice. This is done rapidly.

MEAS. 5—8. Action of Meas. 1—4 is repeated.

### *Part Two.* (MUSIC B)

MEAS. 1—4. As in Part Three of Masquerade, couples take open position with inside hands joined and free hands on waist, and do a step-hop swing apart and together twice while moving forward (counter-clockwise) in the circle. They then take shoulder-waist position and turn with four step-hops, turning clockwise.

MEAS. 5—8. Repeat action of Meas. 1—4. At end, as partners face in original position, they release hands, and each person quickly takes a step to his own left, moving on to a new partner, to begin the dance again.

### *The Words: Part One:*

> *Napoleon was a mighty warrior,*
> *Tra-la-la-la-la-la-la-la-la.*
> *A great big bully fighting terrier,*
> *Tra-la-la-la-la-la-la-la-la.*

### *Part Two:*

> *Oh, Boney fought the Rooshians,*
> *And Boney fought the Prooshians,*
> *And Boney got capitulation!*
> (repeat)

RECORD: Folk Dancer MH-1054B; Educational Dance Recordings FD-2.

# All-American Promenade

Aptly named is this march-like dance, originated by "Doc" Alumbaugh of Arcadia, California, and fitted to a medley of popular old tunes.*

*Formation:* Double circle of couples, facing counter-clockwise, ladies on partner's right, in open position.

### Part One

MEAS. 1—2. Beginning with the outside foot, walk four steps forward (counter-clockwise). On the fourth step, release hands, turn *toward* partner to face clockwise, join new inside hands (man's left, lady's right), and walk backward four steps (still counter-clockwise). Do *not* turn now.

MEAS. 3—4. Repeat action of Meas. 1—2, in reverse direction. Walk four steps forward (clockwise), turn, join inside hands, and walk four steps backward (still clockwise).

### Part Two

MEAS. 5. With inside hands joined, free hand on waist, each couple balances apart and together (modified pas de bas).

MEAS. 6. Lady does a left-face turn, crossing in front of man with four steps, as he crosses behind her, to right, with four steps.

MEAS. 7. Joining inside hands, they balance together and apart.

MEAS. 8. As joined hands are raised, lady does right-face turn under them moving back with four walking steps to meet new partner. Meanwhile, man moves forward to left of next partner.

RECORD: Windsor 7605.

* Used by permission.

# Ten Pretty Girls

This novelty dance may be done in couples, as a mixer, or in groups of three or more dancers in lines moving around the floor. It comes from the American Southwest, and is described here as a couple mixer.

*Formation:* Double circle of couples in open position (inside hands joined, free hands on waist) facing counter-clockwise.

### Part One

MEAS. 1—2. Each person touches the left toe directly in front, then out to the left side, then does a grapevine step to the right, crossing the left foot behind, stepping with the right foot to the side, and crossing the left foot over in front of the right. Pause.

MEAS. 3—4. Action of Meas. 1—2 in reverse: touch right foot in front, to side, and then grapevine to the left: cross right behind, step left to side, and cross right in front of left. Pause.

### Part Two

MEAS. 5—6. Beginning with the left, take four strutting steps forward, in the line of direction: left, right, left, right.

MEAS. 7. Keeping weight on right foot, vigorously swing the left foot forward (leaning body backward), and swing the left foot back (leaning body forward).

MEAS. 8. Releasing partner's hand, each man takes three heavy stamping steps (left-right-left) forward to a new partner, as each lady backs up three steps. He then begins the dance with this new partner, starting with the *right* foot. The leading foot is alternated each time the dance is begun.

NOTE: When done as a threesome mixer, the center person moves forward each time while the other two drop back.

RECORD: MacGregor 605.

# The Roberts

•••••••••••••••••••••••••••••••••••••••••••  SCOTLAND

A fairly simple and slow couple mixer, based on the two-step.

*Formation:* Couples in a double circle, men with backs to center, facing partners. Both hands are joined.

### Part One (MUSIC A)

MEAS. 1—2. Beginning with man's left, lady's right, take two step-draws (slow slides) in the line of direction.

MEAS. 3—4. Each person turns away completely with four steps in the line of direction (man turning to left, lady to right).

MEAS. 5—8. They join both hands again, and repeat action of Meas. 1—4. During the four step turnaway, however, each man moves *forward* to a new partner (the lady ahead of him as he faces in the line of direction).

### Part Two (MUSIC B)

MEAS. 1—2. In open position (inside hands joined, free hand on own waist) each person does a heel-and-toe and one two-step forward, leading with the outside foot.

MEAS. 3—4. Repeat action of Meas. 1—2, with inside foot.

MEAS. 5—8. Partners face and, in closed dance position, do four two-steps, turning clockwise and moving in the line of direction.

RECORD: Rik-Ma-Ree, Beltona 2457; Roberts, Windsor R-607.

# *Teton Mountain Stomp*

Doc Alumbaugh, of Arcadia, California, adapted this dance from the old Buffalo Glide, and it has become a favorite of all age groups.* Even young children can do it, particularly if Part Three is modified as shown.

*Formation:* Single circle of couples with partners facing (men facing counter-clockwise, ladies clockwise) in closed position.

### Part One

MEAS. 1—2. Starting with the man's left, take a side step toward the center, close with right foot, step again with left, and stamp the right foot next to left. Lady does opposite footwork.

MEAS. 3—4. Do same action *away* from center, leading with man's right and lady's left: side-together-side-stamp.

MEAS. 5—6. Man steps with left to side, stamps right, and steps with right to side, and stamps left. Lady does opposite.

### Part Two

MEAS. 7—8. Couples take "banjo" position (Diagram 16), with right sides adjacent. Man walks forward and lady backward, four steps, moving counter-clockwise. On the fourth step, they each do a half right-face turn, so they are in a "sidecar" position, with left sides adjacent.

MEAS. 9—10. Man walks backward and lady forward four steps, still moving counter-clockwise. They take a left-face turn on the fourth step, to face in original direction.

MEAS. 11—12. Releasing partners, they walk forward, passing each other by the right shoulder, and moving on to a new partner with four walking steps.

### Part Three

MEAS. 13—16. Taking closed dance position with this partner, they do two two-steps turning clockwise, and then four pivoting steps, continuing to turn clockwise. End facing in original position, ready to begin the dance again.

NOTE: To simplify the dance, some leaders substitute an eight step buzz swing with the new partner, for Part Three, eliminating the two-step and pivot.

RECORD: Windsor 7615.

* Used by permission.

# Kalvelis

The name of this dance means "little smith," and the actions of the chorus imitate the blacksmith at his forge. Vyts Beliajus introduced Kalvelis to the United States.

*Formation:* Single circle of couples facing the center with hands joined, each lady on her partner's right.

### Part One. (MUSIC A)

MEAS. 1—8 (Repeated). All circle to the right with eight polka steps, and then circle left with eight polkas.

### Chorus. (MUSIC B)

MEAS. 1—2. While facing partner, each person claps his own left hand or fist on his own right hand, then his right hand or fist on his left. Repeat this action.

MEAS. 3—4. Partners link right elbows and turn halfway around (moving clockwise) with two polka steps, starting on the left foot.

MEAS. 5—8. Action of Meas. 1—4 is repeated, with four claps, and a *left*-elbow turn to place.

MEAS. 1—8 (Repeated). Repeat action of Meas. 1—8.

### Part Two. (MUSIC A)

MEAS. 1—4. Ladies move forward to the center with three light polka steps and then stamp three times quickly. They turn and come back to place with three polkas and three stamps.

MEAS. 5—8. Men repeat action of Meas. 1—4, with heavier polka steps. Then do entire CHORUS.

### Part Three. (MUSIC A)

MEAS. 1—8. Partners face, join right hands, and do a grand right and left around the circle, with sixteen polka steps. They meet a new partner and do the entire CHORUS with this person.

NOTE: Additional figures of the dance may include having the ladies weave to the right with sixteen polka steps as the men remain in place, and then do the CHORUS with a new partner. Men then would weave to the right, and do the CHORUS with their original partners. This is done between Parts Two and Three. At the end of the dance (after Part Three), each dancer may do a turning couple polka around the floor with his new partner. The Lithuanian polka is marked by short running steps close to the floor, without a pronounced hop.

RECORD: Folk Dancer MH-1016B; Educational Dance Recordings FD-3.

# Ve'David

.......................................... I S R A E L

This popular Israeli couple mixer, recently originated by Rivkah Sturman, is titled "Ve'David Y'Fey Enayim" (And David of the Beautiful Eyes). It is similar to a number of English and American dances, like Circassian Circle and Oh Susannah.

*Formation:* Double circle of couples facing counter-clockwise with inside hands joined, each lady on her partner's right.

**Part One.** (MUSIC A)

MEAS. 1—2. After a six-measure introduction, all walk forward four steps (starting with the right foot), turning to face the center and join hands in a single circle on the fourth step. All walk backward, away from the center, with four steps.

MEAS. 3—4. Leading with the right foot, all take four steps forward to the center, and four steps backward.

**Part Two.** (MUSIC B)

MEAS. 1—2. As the men clap hands, ladies take four steps to center, and four steps back to place.

MEAS. 3—4. Clapping hands, men walk four steps to the center, turn to the right, and walk away from the center four steps, moving to the lady on their partner's right.

MEAS. 5—6. Taking this lady as his new partner, each man places his right arm around her waist and left arm up in the air, as she does the same. They swing with eight "buzz" steps. The dance is begun again immediately.

RECORD: Folkraft 1432.

# Oslo Waltz

**· · · · · · · · · · · · · · · · · · · · · · · · · · · · · · · · ·** SCOTCH-ENGLISH

This old-time dance is said to be of Scotch-English origin, set to a Norwegian folk melody, although some describe it as an American dance of the last century.

*Formation:* Couples with hands joined in a single circle, facing center. Lady on her partner's right.

### Part One. (MUSIC A)

MEAS. 1—2. All do a waltz balance forward (leading with man's left foot and lady's right) toward the center, and back, with the other foot.

MEAS. 3—4. Man releases his partner's hand, but holds the right hand of the lady on his left. She crosses in front of him with a right-face turn, in two waltz steps (six steps) and ends on his right side, facing center.

MEAS. 5—8, and MEAS. 1—8 (Repeated). Action of Meas. 1—4 is repeated three more times, so each lady has passed to the right *four* times.

### Part Two. (MUSIC A)

MEAS. 1—2. Each man joins both hands with the lady now on his right, his new partner. They do a step-swing balance in waltz rhythm toward the center (man stepping on left foot, swinging right over, and lady with opposite footwork) and then do the same action away from the center.

MEAS. 3—4. Releasing hands, they do a complete turn away from each other in six steps, man turning left and lady right, and moving toward the center.

MEAS. 5—8. Facing and joining hands again, they repeat action of Meas. 1—8 in opposite direction, doing waltz step-swing away from the center, toward the center, and turning individually away from center.

### Part Three. (MUSIC B)

MEAS. 1—4. Joining both hands again, couples take two step-draws toward the center (not taking the weight on the following foot on the second step-draw) and two step-draws away from the center. They maneuver slightly so the man has his back to the center on the last step-draw.

MEAS. 5—6. In closed dance position, couples do two waltz steps, turning clockwise, and moving around the circle counter-clockwise.

MEAS. 7—8. As man faces center, lady twirls to his right, under their joined hands (his left, her right), with six steps. All join hands in a single circle, facing center, to begin dance again.

NOTE: Meas. 5—8 may simply be done as *four* waltz steps.

RECORD: Folk Dancer MH-3016.

## Susan's Gavotte

This dance, composed by Susan Gentry of Oklahoma, is based on the earlier Badger Gavotte, an old-time round dance. In a slightly different form, it is called Lili Marlene, and is danced to that tune.

*Formation:* Double circle of couples in open position, ladies on partner's right, all facing counter-clockwise.

### Part One. (MUSIC A)

MEAS. 1—2. Beginning with the outside foot, each couple walks four steps forward (counter-clockwise). They join both hands and slide four steps in the same direction.

MEAS. 3—4. They turn, face clockwise, and repeat four walks and four slides in this direction.

### Part Two. (MUSIC B)

MEAS. 1—2. Partners face and join both hands. Man steps on the left foot in place, swinging right foot over in front, and then steps on his right foot, swinging the left foot over, as lady does opposite footwork. Repeat this action.

MEAS. 3—4. Taking closed dance position, and beginning with the man's left and lady's right, walk three steps forward (counter-clockwise). Turn toward partner and point the man's right toe (lady's left) in the reverse direction. This action is then done moving clockwise, beginning with the man's right and lady's left: walk-two-three-point.

### Part Three. (MUSIC B)

MEAS. 5—7. In open position (inside hands joined, free hands on waist) couples travel counter-clockwise, doing a two-step apart (back to back) and together (face to face). This action is done three times.

MEAS. 8. Releasing hands, partners turn away in a small circle (man to left and lady to right) with four walking steps. Man moves ahead to next lady, taking her as his new partner, to begin the dance with again.

RECORD: MacGregor 1010; Broadcast 416.

# Klumpakojis

Michael Herman points out that this dance is often wrongly translated as meaning "wooden shoes," but that it should mean "wooden" or "clumsy-footed." Similar dances, like the Swedish Klappdans, are found in many other countries.

*Formation:* Couples in open position in double circle, facing counter-clockwise, lady on right of man.

### Part One. (MUSIC A) ·

MEAS. 1—4. Starting with outside foot, march spiritedly forward (counter-clockwise) for eight steps, turning toward partner on the last count.

MEAS. 5—8. Release joined hands, turn toward partner, join new inside hands (man's left, lady's right), and march eight steps clockwise.

MEAS. 1—8 (Repeated). Partners join right hands (elbows bent, fingers pointing up). Free hand is on waist. They walk around each other clock-wise for eight steps, turn, join left hands, and walk counter-clockwise for eight steps.

### Part Two. (MUSIC B)

MEAS. 1—4. Listen to musical phrase of first two measures, and then clap own hands three times on the accented three beats. Listen again to the phrase, and stamp feet three times to the accented beats.

MEAS. 5—8. Partners shake right forefingers (Diagram 38) at each other three times; repeat with left forefingers. They turn individually with two walking steps (left-face turn) lightly clapping right hands against each other as they turn, and stamp three times in place.

MEAS. 1—8 (Repeated). Repeat action of Meas. 1—8.

### Part Three. (MUSIC C)

MEAS. 1—8 (Repeated twice). In Varsovienne position each couple does eight light polka steps forward, accenting the last with three little stamps. Again they do eight polka steps forward, with the man releasing his partner and moving forward to a new lady on the seventh and eighth steps.

*Diagram 38*

NOTE: This dance is useful for practicing a forward two-step or polka, but may also be done with a walking step or skip for younger children.

RECORD: Columbia 16083F; RCA Victor, LPM 1624.

# Dances for Three

*THERE ARE MANY* lively and enjoyable folk dances which are performed in groups of three—either two men and one lady, two ladies and one man, or with all three of either sex. These dances are especially appropriate in classes or dance clubs where there is a preponderance of one sex or the other, since they enable twenty of one sex to dance very happily with ten of the other. The only problem presented is that when a threesome dance is presented as a mixer, usually with the center person moving on to the next group each time the dance is done, the dancers may be surprised to find themselves in all-male or all-female sets. If they are warned of this in advance and it is treated in a lightly humorous manner, it need not cause concern.

In addition to the threesomes described in this chapter, there are several others ("The Wheat," "Come Let Us Be Joyful," and "Maitelitza") in Chapter Six. "Ten Pretty Girls," in Chapter Ten, may also be done as a threesome dance.

# *Troika*

•••••••••••••••••••••••••••••••••••••••• RUSSIA

The name of this spirited Russian dance is translated as "three horses." It suggests a team of horses pulling a carriage or sleigh at a rapid pace.

*Formation:* Threes facing counter-clockwise, with inside hands joined at shoulder height. The free, outside hands may be extended at shoulder height, or may be placed at the dancers' waists.

## *Part One.* (MUSIC A)

MEAS. 1. Starting with the right foot, take four running steps (somewhat extended, so they are almost leaps) diagonally forward and to the right.

MEAS. 2. Take four similar steps, diagonally forward and to the left.

MEAS. 3—4. Eight similar steps, straight forward in the line of direction.

## *Part Two.* (MUSIC B)

MEAS. 1—2. Keeping hands joined as in Part One, the person on the right runs in front of the center person, under an arch formed by the joined hands of the center person and the left-hand partner, and returns to place. This takes eight steps. Meanwhile, the center person turns left, following her around, under the joined hands.

MEAS. 3—4. Left-hand person repeats this action, running with eight steps under the arch formed by the center person and the right-hand partner, and back to place, while the center person does a right-face turn under the joined hands.

## *Part Three.* (MUSIC C)

MEAS. 1—4. Each threesome joins hands in a small circle and runs twelve steps to the left (clockwise) and stamps three times (left-right-left, and pause).

MEAS. 5—8. Keeping hands joined, they circle right (counter-clockwise) with twelve running steps, and stamp three times (right-left-right, pause), to complete the dance.

NOTE: Part One is often done with high kicking steps, rather than runs. While not authentic, dancers enjoy doing it this way—if they have the energy. Part Three *may* end with the center person moving forward to the next group, to begin the dance again with them.

RECORD: Folk Dancer MH-1059 (Fast); Educational Dance Recordings FD-2.

# Norwegian Mountain March

•••••••••••••••••••••••••••••••••• NORWAY

*Diagram 39*

This dance suggests two mountain climbers led by a guide over rough terrain.

*Formation:* Groups of three, with the center person in front and the other two slightly behind, all facing counter-clockwise. They may simply hold hands, or may be linked by handkerchiefs or scarves (Diagram 39).

*Part One.* (MUSIC A)

MEAS. 1—8. Beginning with the right foot, take eight running waltz steps forward, lightly accenting the first step of each measure. The center person looks over his shoulder at his partners, first one and then the other.

*Part Two.* (MUSIC A)

MEAS. 1—2. The center person moves backward under the joined, raised hands of the other two, with two running waltz steps, while the two end dancers take the same steps in place.

MEAS. 3—4. The dancer on the left, moving clockwise, travels across in front of the center person and under his right arm, with two running waltz steps. The others step in place.

MEAS. 5—6. The dancer on the right makes a left-face turn under the center person's right arm, with two running waltz steps.

MEAS. 7—8. The center person makes a right-face turn under his own right arm, bringing the group back to the original formation.

MEAS. 1—8 (Repeated). Repeat action of Meas. 1—8, Part Two.

NOTE: It is important *not* to let go of the scarves at any time throughout the dance, so Part Two should be carefully practiced before it is done with the music. A slow step hop may be used, instead of the running waltz.

RECORD: RCA Victor LPM 1622; Educational Dance Recordings FD-1.

## *Alfelder*

...................................... GERMANY

This German folk dance for three, first taught in the United States by Gretel and Paul Dunsing, is much like "Come Let Us Be Joyful."

*Formation:* Threes facing threes in a large circle around the room. One three faces clockwise, the other counter-clockwise.

### *Part One.* (MUSIC A)

MEAS. 1—8 (Repeated). Joining hands in a circle, all six dancers take eight slow walking steps to the left, then eight steps to the right, returning to place.

(MUSIC B)

MEAS. 1—8 (Repeated). The center persons in each group of three move forward, hook right elbows with each other and turn clockwise with four walking steps. He returns to his *right-hand* partner, hooks left elbows with her and turns counter-clockwise with four steps. He joins right elbows with his *left-hand* partner and turns her clockwise with four steps, and returns to his original position with four steps.

MEAS. 1—8 (Repeated). Keeping hands joined in lines of three, each person bows or curtseys to the opposite group in four counts. Each group walks diagonally forward and to the right, passing the opposite three, with eight steps. Each group moves into position to face the next three, and bows to them in four counts.

RECORD: Methodist World of Fun M-115.

# Dashing White Sergeant

•••••••••••••••••••••••••••••••••••••• SCOTLAND

Michael Herman points out that the basic step used in this dance, the "skip-change-step," is difficult to execute correctly without much practice in Scottish country dancing. He suggests that a light polka step, with the toe leading and the instep of the following foot brought up under the leading heel, will resemble the "skip-change-step" and may be substituted for it.

*Formation:* Threes facing threes in a large circle around the floor. One three faces clockwise, the other counter-clockwise.

### Part One. (MUSIC A)

MEAS. 1—8. Joining hands in a circle, all six dancers take eight light sliding steps to the left, and then eight to the right. They end in their original lines of three.

### Part Two. (MUSIC A)

MEAS. 1—2. In each set of three, the center person faces the person on his right. They each do a pas de bas step to the right and then to the left.

MEAS. 3—4. The center person joins both hands with this right-hand partner; they turn once with two light polka steps, moving clockwise completely around each other and back to place.

MEAS. 5—8. The center person faces his *left*-hand partner and repeats this action with her: pas de bas to the right, to the left, and then a two hand turn with two polka steps.

### Part Three. (MUSIC B)

MEAS. 1—8. The center person faces his *right*-hand partner again. All three dancers do a "Reel of Three," or "Figure Eight." This is very similar to the last action of "Black Nag," (pg. 183), often called "Shepherd's Hey." Each dancer describes a figure eight with eight light polka steps. The center person and his right-hand partner begin by moving to the right, so they are passing *left* shoulders, moving around the loop of the "figure eight" and into the center (Diagram 42). The left-hand person waits for a count or two (so he does not collide with the right-hand person) and then starts on *his* figure eight, moving to the left to begin. They then all continue to move simultaneously, until they are back in their starting positions.

*Diagram 42*

**Part Four.** (MUSIC C)

MEAS. 1—4. Taking the starting position, with hands joined in lines of three, the lines move foward toward each other with two light polka steps, and backward with two polka steps.

MEAS. 5—8. Releasing hands, the lines move forward with four polka steps, passing through each other (each person passes right shoulders with the dancer directly opposite him) and moving on to face a new group, to begin the dance again with them.

RECORD: Imperial 1005, RCA Victor LPM 1619; Educational Dance Recordings FD-4.

# *Raksi Jaak*

......................................... ESTONIA

*Diagram 43*

This infectious dance (introduced by Alice Zimmerman of the Estonian Society of Folk Dance House in New York City) was learned by the author at the College of the Pacific Folk Dance Camp in California shortly thereafter, as taught by Walter Grothe. Folk dances travel!

*Formation*: Sets of threes, standing side by side with each other, inside hands joined and free hands at sides. All face the *center* of the circle.

### *Chorus.* (MUSIC A)

MEAS. 1—4. Each dancer steps to the left with his left foot, and brings his right foot up to it, then steps to the right with his right foot, bringing the left foot up to it. This is repeated.

MEAS. 5—8. Each dancer walks three steps forward, toward the center (left, right, left) and kicks his right foot forward, with the knee straight. He walks backward four steps to place, starting with the right foot.

**Part One.** (MUSIC B)

MEAS. 1—8. Using short, bouncy polka steps throughout, the two outside dancers move at the same time, crossing over in front of the center dancer. The right-hand dancer goes *over*, the left-hand dancer *under*. They continue forward and around the center person, crossing again in back, with the person who went over before now going under, and vice-versa. Meanwhile the center person continues to face forward, holding his joined hands overhead, maintaining light contact with the hands of the others. This entire action is repeated. Then do CHORUS.

**Part Two.** (MUSIC B)

MEAS. 1—4. On the last two counts of the Chorus, the two end dancers have turned to face the center dancer, so their backs are to the center of the circle. All hands are joined in this position, with arms extended straight. All take four polka steps toward the center, with the center person moving forward, the others moving backward.

MEAS. 5—8. As the center person takes four polka steps backward to place, he holds his hands high. The outer dancers release each other's hand, but hold *his*, and twirl inward, turning twice with four polka steps (right-hand person makes left-face turn, and left-hand person makes right-face turn). Then do CHORUS.

**Part Three.** (MUSIC B)

MEAS. 1—4. On the last two counts of the Chorus, the outer dancers "tuck-in," by turning completely toward the center person, and facing the center. His hands are now behind their backs and they are close together (Diagram 43). In this position, all do four polka steps forward, to the center.

MEAS. 5—6. All take two polka steps backward to place.

MEAS. 7—8. The center person takes two more steps backward to place, as the other two "unwind" by twirling outward with two polka steps under the still-joined hands.

Then do CHORUS.

NOTE: Ella Noormets, a dance teacher from Estonia studying at Teachers College, Columbia, suggests that there is a very simple figure which may be used to precede the others (making four Parts in all), in which the threesome simply takes four polka steps forward, and four backward.

RECORD: Folk Dancer MH-3007.

# Three Man Schottische

Also called the "Texas Schottische for Three," this is a relaxed mixer—much less strenuous than the "Troika."

*Formation:* Threes face counter-clockwise in the large circle. The center person has hands joined with the other two; they join hands behind his back (Diagram 40).

### Part One

MEAS. 1—2. Each threesome moves forward with two two-steps: left-right-left, pause, right-left-right, pause.

MEAS. 3—4. They continue forward with four slow walking steps: left, right, left, right.

### Part Two

MEAS. 5. Each person places his left heel forward on the floor, pauses, then touches his left toe to the floor in front of his right foot. Pause.

MEAS. 6. As the center person takes three steps in place, the other two release each other's hands and walk forward three steps (left-right-left) turning to face the center person. They still hold his hands (Diagram 41).

MEAS. 7. Each person places his right heel forward, pauses, and touches his right toe to the floor. Pause.

MEAS. 8. The center person takes three steps forward, moving counter-clockwise (right-left-right), at the same time pulling the other two past him (they move clockwise with three steps). Each center person has thus moved on to a new pair of outside dancers; they join hands in the starting position to begin the dance.

RECORDS "Oklahoma Mixer," Educational Dance Recordings FD-3; or any good American Schottische.

(*top*)   Diagram 40
(*left*)   Diagram 41

## Polka Zu Drien

This is a fairly simple threesome dance that gives good opportunity to practice the polka.

**FORMATION:** Groups of three, with inside hands joined, all facing counter-clockwise.

### Chorus. (MUSIC A)
MEAS. 1—2. Each person touches his right heel forward, toe up, and leaning back. He touches his right toe to the floor, slightly behind the other foot, and leans forward. He takes one polka step forward with the right foot leading.

MEAS. 3—4. The same action, heel-and-toe and polka step, is done with the left foot leading.

MEAS. 5—8. Repeat the action of Meas. 1—4, but on the eighth measure, instead of taking a polka step forward, each person releases hands and turns individually in place with three steps, to face clockwise.

MEAS. 1—8 (Repeated). The action of Meas. 1—8 is repeated, moving clockwise. At the end, each dancer turns again, so the threes are facing counter-clockwise, as at the beginning.

### Part One. (MUSIC B)

MEAS. 1—8. Dancers join right hands, in star formation, in their own groups of three. They do eight polka steps, moving clockwise in the star.

MEAS. 1—8 (Repeated). Dancers now join left hands in the star formation and do eight polka steps counter-clockwise.

They open up to face forward again, and do the CHORUS.

### Part Two. (MUSIC B)

MEAS. 1—8. They join hands in circles of three and move to the left (clockwise) with eight polka steps.

MEAS. 1—8 (Repeated). With hands still joined, they do eight polka steps to the right (counter-clockwise).

Facing forward in original formation, they do the CHORUS.

**RECORD:** Folk Dancer MH-1050.

# Longways Dances

............................................ *12*

THE FAMED DANCE historian, Curt Sachs, points out in his "World History of the Dance" that the two basic types of dance formation since the Early Stone Age, have been the circle and the line, or longways formation. The chief collection of English dances, John Playford's "English Dancing Master," describes in its final edition (1728) nine hundred country dances, most of them in either the circle or longways formation.

This chapter includes a variety of English, Irish, French, and American longways dances which are suitable for instruction in schools, colleges and recreation groups—including a good selection of American *contra dances*. They all have this basic ingredient: they are performed with the men and women in straight lines facing each other. In general, too, it is safe to say about them that they involve little in the way of footwork, but are interesting and challenging because of their movement patterns, and ways of progressing "down the set." These are described on the following pages.

# The Minuet

*Diagram 44*

This French court dance, introduced at the time of Louis XIV, was popular both throughout Europe and in the American colonies during the 18th Century. It is a courtly, slow dance, with many deep bows and curtseys, and is often done with school children.

*Formation*: Longways formation, with even number of couples (six or eight are best). Each boy holds his partner's left hand in his right, and they face forward, toe of inside foot extended (Diagram 44).

### Part One. (MUSIC A)

MEAS. 1—2. Beginning with the inside foot, take three slow walking steps forward, then point the free (outside) foot forward and hold for two more counts. This is known as a minuet step: step-step-step, point-two-three.

MEAS. 3—6. Take two more minuet steps forward, leading with the outside and then inside feet.

MEAS. 7—8. Partners face and bow or curtsey deeply for six counts.

MEAS. 1—8. (Repeated). Partners turn in place to face in opposite direction, join new inside hands, and repeat action of Meas. 1—8, in this direction.

### Part Two. (MUSIC B)

MEAS. 1—4. Partners face, join right hands, and balance forward and back. They step forward on the right foot, rise up slightly on the ball of the foot, step back on the left foot, and point the right toe forward. This action is repeated.

MEAS. 5—8. Keeping right hands joined, partners exchange places, crossing over in six steps (beginning with the right foot) and bow or curtsey deeply for six counts.

MUSIC 1—8 (Repeated). Repeat action of Meas. 1—8, returning to place.

NOTE: There are many different variations of the Minuet, including a third figure in which sets of two couples (1st and 2nd, 3rd and 4th, etc.) do a right-hand star and then a left-hand star. The dance is quite slow throughout, and the author has actually played the RCA Victor 33⅓ r.p.m. record at 45 r.p.m., to speed it up; children have found this tempo quite comfortable.

RECORD: Folkraft 1179; RCA Victor LPM 1621.

## Galopede

•••••••••••••••••••••••••••••••••••••••••••  ENGLAND

Many of the traditional English country dances were, unlike the Minuet, spirited and bouncy. They tended to be casual, friendly, democratic dances in the sense that anyone could take part, without special training. Galopede is a good example of these.

*Formation*: Longways formation of four to six couples, men in one line facing ladies in the other.

*Part One.* (MUSIC A)

MEAS. 1—4. With hands joined in lines, all walk forward three steps, bow or curtsey to partner, and walk backward four steps.

MEAS. 5—8. Dropping hands, the lines cross over. Each person changes places with his partner, passing right shoulders and turning to the right to face her, in eight steps.

MEAS. 1—8 (Repeated). Repeat action of Meas. 1—8.

*Part Two.* (MUSIC B)

MEAS. 1—8. Partners join both hands and swing in place, turning clockwise with sixteen skips, or eight polka steps. The term "reel" is sometimes used to describe a light, lifting polka step.

MEAS. 1—8 (Repeated). The first couple continues to swing, moving down between the lines to the "foot" of the set, with sixteen skips or eight turning polkas, while the others clap hands and move one position up toward the "head" of the set.

NOTE: Each time the dance is done, a new first couple swings down the center of the set. This is typical of the "Virginia Reel," and in slightly different form, other contra dances.

RECORD: Folkraft 1331.

## *The Rifleman*

*Diagram 45*

This dance is similar to, but slightly more difficult than "Galopede." It presents an interesting variation of the "ladies chain" figure.

*Formation:* An even number of couples in a line facing a similar number in the opposite line; each lady on her partner's right (Diagram 45).

*Part One.* (MUSIC A)

MEAS. 1—4. With hands joined in lines, all take two polka (reel) steps forward, and two backward.

MEAS. 5—8. Releasing his own partner's hand, each person advances again, joins both hands with the opposite person (in promenade position) and leads her around counter-clockwise to place in his line, with four polka steps.

MEAS. 1—8 (Repeated). Repeat action of Meas. 1—8. Everyone is now in original positions.

*Part Two.* (MUSIC B)

MEAS. 1—4. Ladies chain across in this manner: they go forward, give right hands to each other, pass by, and give left hands to the opposite man. He does not turn, but helps her do a half right-face twirl under their joined hands, and passes her behind him. As she comes over to his right side, he takes her left hand in his right. This is done with four polka steps.

MEAS. 5—8. Ladies chain back to their original partners in the same way.

### Part Three

MEAS. 1—8 (Repeated). The first two couples in each line take closed dance position (each with his own partner) and do a turning polka step, side by side, moving down between the lines to the foot of the set. The other couples move one position up the set, clapping. This is done with eight polka steps.

RECORD: Folkraft F1114.

## *Virginia Reel*

•••••••••••••••••••••••••••••••••••••••••• UNITED STATES

There are many versions of this dance, which is known as the most popular of all American country dances. Actually, it is descended from an English dance, Sir Roger de Coverley. Here is the sequence, as the author usually calls it.

**Formation:** Four to eight couples in longways formation, men facing ladies. The best number of couples is usually five or six.

### Part One. (MUSIC A)

MEAS. 1—8. Men join hands in their line and ladies in theirs. All walk forward four steps and backward four steps. Repeat this.

(MUSIC B)

MEAS. 1—8. All walk forward, join right hands with partners, turn once clockwise, and return to place. Do the same with left hands joined, turning counter clockwise.

(MUSIC A)

MEAS. 1—8. Walk forward, join both hands with partners and turn once clockwise, returning to place. All walk forward and do-si-do, passing right shoulders and moving back-to-back, and passing left shoulders as they back up to place.

**Part Two.** (MUSIC B)

MEAS. 1—8. The first couple in each set becomes active. They join both hands and slide, or "sashay," eight slides down the center of the set, and eight slides back to place.

(MUSIC C)

MEAS. 1—8 (Repeated). The first couple does the "reel." They hook right elbows with each other and turn one and a half times, clockwise. They then go to the opposite line (man to the ladies' line and vice versa) and turn the next person there with a left elbow hook. They meet each other in the center again, turn with a right elbow. They go to the *next* person in the opposite line again, and turn with a left elbow. This "reeling" action is continued until the first couple has reached the foot of the set, and may take more or less music, depending on the number of couples in the line. They then join both hands with each other and slide up to the head of their respective lines.

**Part Three.** (MUSIC D)

MEAS. 1—8. Facing toward the head of the set, the first man leads to the left and down toward the foot, as the first lady leads to the right and down to the foot. The others follow them.

MEAS. 1—8 (Repeated). The first couple joins both hands in an arch. The others walk below them, and then come up *under* the arch, to re-form their lines, leaving the first couple at the foot of the set. *Only* the first couple makes an arch; the others keep their original order. The dance is repeated as many times as there are couples, each time with a new couple active in Parts Two and Three.

RECORD: RCA Victor LPM-1623 (without calls); RCA Victor LE-3002 (with calls by the author).

## American Contra Dances

The traditional American contra dance of the colonial period and early 19th Century has survived chiefly in New England, although it continues to be done in some square and folk dance groups elsewhere in the United States. It is a unique and interesting form of dance, somewhat similar to square dancing, but with the great dependence on musical phrase that characterizes folk dances as such.

The contra dance is done in longways formation, and has these characteristics.

1. A suitable number of couples in each set is from eight to twelve couples. Usually, the first, third, fifth and all odd couples are *active*, and face *down* the set to begin the dance, while the second, fourth, sixth and all even-numbered couples are *inactive*, and face *up* the set. Each time the action of the dance is completed, active couples move down the set one place, and inactive couples move up, one place, toward the head. When a couple reaches the head or foot of the set, it waits once and then changes its role (actives becoming inactive and vice versa) to begin the dance again, moving in the reverse direction. If the dance is one in which the active couples have crossed over, changing places, in order to begin the dance (as in Lady of the Lake), they must cross over while they are waiting at the head or foot to begin the dance again. There are other types of formations (such as having the first, fourth, seventh and tenth couples active) but these are less common, and are not described here.

2. The contra dance is performed precisely to the music, usually in an AABB form, requiring thirty-two measures to complete the action once. The typical "call" is done in the "prompt" style, in which the call is given on the measures immediately preceding the music which accompanies an action. This means that the dancer has been warned just in time to swing into action on exactly the right beat, and to dance *with the music*. In some cases, the calls are given simultaneously with the action, and if they are simple and familiar enough, this causes no difficulty.

3. While it has a few characteristic movements of its own, contra dancing depends largely on such actions as the *star, balance, swing, ladies chain* and *right* and *left through*, all of which may be practiced in other dances in this book as preparation. Portland Fancy is a useful dance for groups to learn, before starting contra dancing.

# Lady of the Lake

.................................... UNITED STATES

*Diagram 46*

One of the best-loved of the traditional contras, and a good one to begin with.

**Formation.** Longways set of eight to twelve couples. Each odd-numbered couple (one, three, five, etc.) is *active* and crosses over, exchanging places and facing down toward the foot of the set, while *inactive* couples face up toward the head (Diagram 46).

**Part One.** (MUSIC A)

MEAS. 1—8. "*Actives, balance and swing the one below.*" Each active person joins right hands with the inactive person he is facing. They do a step-swing balance, stepping on the right foot and swinging the left foot over, then stepping on the left and swinging the right. (There are other balances, like the pas de bas, or two steps forward and two back, but this is the commonest). Taking closed position with this inactive person, the actives swing with twelve buzz steps.

(MUSIC A)

MEAS. 1—8 (Repeated). *"Actives, balance and swing your partner."* The active couples only repeat the action of Meas. 1—8, with their *own* partners in the center (between the lines).

*Part Two.* (MUSIC B)

MEAS. 1—4. *"Down the set go two by two."* The active couples face down toward the foot of the set (lady on her partner's right), join inside hands and walk six steps forward. On the seventh and eighth counts, they turn individually, face up toward the head, and join inside hands.

MEAS. 5—8. *"Come back up and cast off."* The actives walk up toward the head of the set and, releasing their own partner's hands, separate, man to the right and lady to the left. Placing their free arms around the waist of the inactive person they "cast off," turning about three-quarters with this person, so they now face across the set (Diagram 45), each lady on the right of a man.

MEAS. 1—8 (Repeated). *"Ladies chain."* The two ladies do a ladies chain over and back, as in Portland Fancy (page 127).

NOTE: The dance has been completed once and, because of the "cast off," each active couple has moved one position *down,* and each inactive couple one position *up,* the set. As described on page 167, they continue to dance, facing a new couple each time, until they reach the head or foot of the set. Then they wait while the dance is done *once,* cross over, and dance again in a new role (active becomes inactive, and vice versa).

RECORD: Many good contra dance records are used interchangeably for different dances. Two useful suggestions are: "Reilly's Own," Folk Dancer MH-1072-A and "Garfield's Hornpipe," Folk Dancer MH-1065-B. A record specifically suggested for this dance is Folk Dancer MH-1028-B, "Golden Stairs."

# Haymaker's Jig

......................................

In this lively contra, the action is much like "Lady of the Lake," but the progression of active couples down the set comes in a different way.

*Formation:* Longways formation, with 1st, 3rd, 5th and all odd couples active. They cross over.

### Part One. (MUSIC A)

MEAS. 1—8. "*Actives, balance and swing the one below!*" Active couples face down, join right hands with the person below them in the line, do the step-swing balance, and swing, as in "Lady of the Lake."

MEAS. 1—8 (Repeated). "*Balance and swing your own in the center.*" Active couples only balance and swing.

### Part Two. (MUSIC B)

MEAS. 1—4. "*Go down the center four in line.*" The active couple (with the lady on her partner's right) faces down the set and stands between the inactive couple below them. They join hands in a line of four with them, and march six steps down the set. On the seventh and eighth counts, they turn individually to face up the set, and join hands in a line of four.

MEAS. 5—8. "*Come right back. . . .*" In this line of four, they march six steps up toward the head of the set. On the seventh and eighth counts, each man continues to hold the hand of the girl on his right and the couples thus formed back out to face across the set. The active couples have just moved one position down the set.

MEAS. 1—8 (Repeated). "*. . . and the ladies chain.*" Ladies chain over and back. This completes the dance sequence. Active couples now face down the set, and inactive couples face up, to begin the dance again. As in "Lady of the Lake," the couple that reaches the head or foot of the set waits for one sequence, crosses over, and begins the dance again in a new role.

RECORD: Suggested records: "Reilly's Own," Folk Dancer MH-1072B, "Garfield's Hornpipe," MH-1065B. With calls by the author, try RCA Victor, LE-3004.

# Jefferson's Reel

This contra dance is very similar to one called "Jefferson and Liberty," but has a closing figure that resembles the "Haymaker's Jig." Often contras differ from each in this way—just enough to make them interesting.

*Formation:* Longways formation. Active couples (1st, 3rd, 5th, etc.) do *not* cross over.

### Part One. (MUSIC A)

MEAS. 1—4. *"Circle four with the one below."* Active couples face down, join hands with the inactive couples below them and circle eight walking steps to the left.

MEAS. 5—8. *"Now circle to the right you go."* They circle eight steps back to the right.

MEAS. 1—8 (Repeated). *"Right hand star with the couple below. . . . and back with the left."* The same four people join right hands in a star and walk clockwise eight steps. They turn, make a left hand star and walk counterclockwise eight steps. They return to place in the original lines.

### Part Two. (MUSIC B)

MEAS. 1—4. *"Actives, down the outside all alone. . ."* The active man and lady turn out and walk six steps individually, down the *outside* of their respective lines. On the seventh and eighth counts, they turn, to face up the set.

MEAS. 5—8. *"Come right back and cast off."* Active man and lady walk up the outside of the set and "cast off" around the inactive person who had been below them, coming into the center of the set.

MEAS. 1—4 (Repeated). *"Down the center, four in line."* As in "Haymaker's Jig," they join hands in lines of four (the active lady is on her partner's left) and walk six steps down toward the foot of the set. On the seventh and eighth counts, the active man raises his partner's hand, forming an arch.

MEAS. 5—8 (Repeated). *"Ends duck through, come up the hall."* The inactive man and lady step forward, duck under this arch, (Diagram 49) and all walk eight steps moving toward the head of the set. The active couple now faces a new inactive couple, and is ready to begin the dance.

RECORD: "Glise a Sherbrooke," Folk Dancer MH-10073-B, or any good contra dance tune.

## Petronella

Originally a Scottish longways dance, this became a popular New England contra dance, sometimes affectionately called "Pat'nella."

*Formation:* Longways set. Active couples do *not* cross over.

### Part One. (MUSIC A)

MEAS. 1—2. "*Actives balance in the middle of the hall.*" Facing each other, the active man and lady (first, third, fifth couples, etc.) do a balance. This may be a step swing, or any other form of balance.

MEAS. 3—4. "*Quarter turn to the right with you.*" The active man and lady each do a quarter turn to their own right with four steps, so the man is facing up the set and the lady down.

MEAS. 5—6. "*Balance up and down the set.*" They balance, as in Meas. 1—2 (using different steps, if they wish).

MEAS. 7—8. "*And quarter turn to the right again.*" Each active dancer again does a quarter turn to his right with four steps, so they have crossed over; the man has his back to the ladies' line and vice versa.

MEAS. 1—8 (Repeated). Repeat action of Meas. 1—8, back to place (Diagram 47).

### Part Two. (MUSIC B)

MEAS. 1—4. "*Down the center, two by two . . .*" As in "Lady of the Lake," active couples walk down the set. They turn individually on the seventh and eighth counts, to face up.

**Diagram 47**

MEAS. 5—8. *"Come right back and cast off."* Marching back up, the man "casts off" to his *left*, around the inactive man who had been below him, while the lady casts off to her *right*, around the lady.

MEAS. 1—8 (Repeated). *"Right and left through with the couple above."* Each active man and the man he has just cast off with act as a couple, as the ladies do the same. They do a right and left through across the set and back as in Portland Fancy (page 126), with the person on the right in each couple turning as a lady, and the one on the left turning as a man, in the courtesy turn.

RECORD: Folk Dancer MH-1067.

## Hull's Victory

UNITED STATES

This traditional old contra dance was originally danced to celebrate the victory of Captain Isaac Hull and his Frigate "Constitution" in a naval battle with the British, during the War of 1812.

*Formation:* Longways formation. Active couples (1st, 3rd, 5th, etc.) do *not* cross over.

*Part One.* (MUSIC A)

MEAS. 1—2. *"Right hand to partner, left to the opposite. . ."* Each active man and lady walks forward with four steps. They join right hands (and continue to hold this hand) and pass each other, taking left hands with the opposite person, in the inactive couple below them. Men now face down the set, and ladies up toward the head (Diagram 48).

*Diagram 48*

MEAS. 3—4. ". . . *and balance four in line.*" Each person in this line of four takes two steps forward, and two backward.

MEAS. 5—8. "*Turn with the left hand twice around.*" The active person releases his partner's hand and turns the inactive person whose left hand he is holding *twice* around, counter-clockwise.

MEAS. 1—4 (Repeated). "*Right hand to partner, go once around, and balance four in line once more.*" Releasing the inactive person's hand, the active dancers go into the center, join right hands with each other and turn once clockwise with four steps, coming back into the line of four. Just as in Meas. 3—4, they balance forward and back again.

MEAS. 5—8 (Repeated). "*Active couples swing in the middle.*" In closed dance position, active couples swing with eight buzz steps.

*Part Two.* (MUSIC B)

MEAS. 1—4. "*Go down the center, two by two, turn as a couple, come back with you . . .*" With the lady on the right of her partner, and with inside hands joined, the active couples walk six steps down the set. On counts seven and eight, they turn as a couple, facing up the set, lady on the right.

MEAS. 5—8. "*Come back up and don't be slow, cast off with the couple below.*" The active couple walk back up the set and "cast off," lady around the inactive lady who had been below her, and man around the inactive man.

MEAS. 1—8 (Repeated). "*Right and left through and right and left back.*" As in the last part of "Petronella," the two men, acting as a couple, do a right and left through over, and back, with the two ladies, also acting as a couple. Each active person has moved one position down the set and now turns to face the next inactive person below, to begin the dance again.

RECORD: Folk Dancer MH-1065-A.

# Waves of Tory

Most Irish exhibition folk dancing tends to be extremely difficult, based on quick step-movements which are very much like tap dancing and require long training to do well. There are a number of Irish longways dances, however, which are similar in pattern to English and American dances, and which have only a few special actions which must be learned. These include the Side Step ("Sevens" and "Threes") and the Promenade Step, which are described as they appear. The dance, "Waves of Tory," is named after the rough seas beating against the island of Tory, off the coast of Donegal, and the "over and under" action of Part Two suggests these waves.

*Formation:* Longways formation with an even number of couples, preferably six or eight, men on one side, ladies on the other.

### Part Three. (MUSIC A, Repeated)

MEAS. 1—4. *"Lead up"* and *"retire."* With hands joined in lines, each person goes forward toward his partner with two Promenade steps, and "retires," moving backward with two Promenade steps. (The Promenade is like a two-step: step forward with the right foot, bring the left toe to the right heel, step forward again on the right and come up slightly on the ball of the right foot, lifting the left foot from the floor. Repeat with the left foot leading.)

MEAS. 5—6. *"Lead up"* again, with the lines taking two Promenade steps forward.

MEAS. 7—8. *Two "Threes" in place.* (Place the ball of the right foot directly behind the left foot, lifting the left foot slightly. Step on the left foot in place, lifting the right foot slightly. Step on the right foot and pause. This is done very quickly. The second "Three" is done in the same way, but with the left foot placed behind the right, to begin).

MEAS. 1—8 (Repeated). Each odd couple joins right hands with the couple below it in the set (1st with 2nd, 3rd with 4th, etc.), making a right hand star. They do four Promenade steps moving clockwise. They turn in, join left hands, and do four Promenade steps moving counter-clockwise in a left-hand star. As this is completed, they drop back to their original places in the lines.

(MUSIC B)

MEAS. 1—8, and 1—8 (Repeated). The entire action done thus far is repeated: "lead up" and "retire," "lead up" again, two "Threes" in place, followed by a *left*-hand star, and then a *right*-hand star.

*Part Two.* (MUSIC A)

MEAS. 1—8. "*Lead to the right.*" Partners join inside hands, facing toward the head of the set. The first couple leads to the right and down toward the foot of the set. As the other couples follow them, with Promenade steps, they reach the foot, turn and come up the center again, resuming the original formation.

MEAS. 1—8. (With added music as needed). "*The Waves.*" All the odd-numbered couples face down the set, raising inside hands high to make arches. The even-numbered couples face up the set. They all move forward with an "over and under action," alternately going *over* a couple and then *under* a couple. Odd couples begin by going over; even couples by going under. When a couple reaches the end of the set, it turns and comes back. This is continued, using Promenade steps, until each couple is back in its starting position.

*Part Three.* (MUSIC A, repeated)

MEAS. 1—8. "*Cast off, form an arch and all go through.*" The first lady casts off to the right and the man to the left. As the others in their lines follow them, using Promenade steps throughout, the first couple forms an arch and the others go through. They form their original lines, leaving the first couple at the foot, just as in the Virginia Reel.

NOTE: When the dance is begun again, unlike American contra dances, every couple has changed its role. The old 2nd couple is now the 1st, the 3rd couple is now the 2nd, etc., and they must be alert, particularly when it comes to the "Waves" figure.

RECORD: Rakes of Mallow, Capitol 10250; Folk Dancer Album FD-22.

# The Bridge of Athlone

Another interesting Irish dance in the longways formation, this uses several of the same steps found in "Waves of Tory."

*Formation:* Longways, just as in "Waves of Tory."

### Part One. (MUSIC A)

MEAS. 1—4. The two lines, with hands joined, take two Promenade steps forward, beginning right, and two backward.

MEAS. 5—8. Repeat action of Meas. 1—4.

MEAS. 1—4 (Repeated). *"Sevens" and "Threes."* (To do the "Sevens," each dancer travels to his own right, while facing directly forward. He steps behind his right foot with his left (one), steps right to the side (two), steps behind with the left (three), steps right to the side (four), behind with the left (five), right to the side (six), and behind with the left (seven) lifting the right foot and pausing. This is done with quick, short steps, by the entire line, with hands joined. Immediately, each dancer does two "Threes," right-left-right, left-right-left, in place (see "Waves of Tory").

MEAS. 5—8 (Repeated). Each dancer does the "Sevens" and "Threes" to his left, starting with the right foot cutting behind the left.

### Part Two. (MUSIC B)

MEAS. 1—2. The first couple only joins both hands. They do the Side Step ("Seven" only) traveling down the set to the man's right and lady's left, while facing each other.

MEAS. 3—4. They turn halfway to the right in place, with two "Threes," so the man now faces the men's line and vice versa.

MEAS. 5—8. Repeat action of Meas. 9—12, *up* the set with "Seven" and crossing over to place with two "Threes."

### Part Three

MEAS. 1—8 (Repeated). *"Cast Off."* First couple separates, lady to the right and man to the left, and goes down to the foot with eight Promenade steps, as the others follow them.

(MUSIC A)

MEAS. 1—8. *"Form the Bridge."* The first couple joins both hands and makes an arch, through which other couples go straight up to their original places, leaving the first couple at the foot. Every other couple in the set now joins both hands, making a long "bridge."

MEAS. 1—8 (Repeated). *"Lady under, man outside."* The first couple releases hands and does eight Promenade steps up the set, lady going *under* the bridge and man passing on the *outside* (left side) of the bridge.

(MUSIC B)

MEAS. 1—8. *"Man under, lady outside."* When they reach the head of the set, the first man and lady turn to the right, and go *down* the set with Promenade steps. The man now goes *under* the bridge, and the lady down the outside (right side) of the bridge. They remain at the foot of the set, as the dance is begun again.

RECORD: Any good Irish reel, as in "Waves of Tory."

## Oxdans

••••••••••••••••••••••••••••••••••••••••••   S W E D E N

This dance, which represents a humorous mock battle, is performed only by men or boys. It is said to have originated at the college in Karlstad, Sweden, where freshmen (called "Oxen" by upper-classmen) were required to dance it without smiling—in spite of its ludicrous actions. It is also called "Oxen Dance" or "Oxdansen."

*Formation:* It may be performed by two boys facing each other, or by two facing lines of boys or men. One line of boys will be called One, and the opposite line, Two.

*Introduction:* MEAS. 1—8. This is the same music that is used for the CHORUS, but since it is played without any other introduction, the dancers may simply wait in starting position with hands on hips, fingers pointing forward, heels together, toes apart.

*Part One.* (MUSIC A)

MEAS. 1. Dancers stand still.

MEAS. 2. Each Number One, with knees straight, bows deeply while his partner, Number Two, bends both knees in a deep squat position. They resume starting position on the second count of the measure.

MEAS. 3. Dancers stand still.

MEAS. 4. Number Two bows as Number One does the squat. They return to position.

MEAS. 5—8. Action of Meas. 1—4 is repeated.

MEAS. 9. Number One does a quick bow, while Number Two squats. Then Number Two bows, while Number One does the squat.

MEAS. 10—16. Action of Meas. 9 is repeated rapidly seven more times.

### Chorus. (MUSIC B)

MEAS. 1. Partners face each other with fists clenched in front of their own chests, elbows out to the side, shoulders high. Turning his head to the right, Number One takes a wide side-step to his right, at the same time flinging his arms, fists still clenched, out to the side. He closes with the left foot. (Number Two does exactly the same action, moving to his left, "mirroring" Number One throughout the CHORUS).

MEAS. 2. Number One steps with the right foot to the side, and stamps with his left foot in place, at the same time bringing his fists back in front of his chest with a quick snap, and facing his partner.

MEAS. 3—4. Repeat this action, moving to Number One's left.

MEAS. 5—8. Repeat action of Meas. 1—4.

### Part Two. (MUSIC A)

MEAS. 1. Dancers stand still, hands on hips.

MEAS. 2. Each dancer springs in place on his left foot, placing the right foot forward, without taking weight.

MEAS. 3. Stand still in this position.

MEAS. 4. Spring in place on right foot, placing left foot forward.

MEAS. 5—8. Repeat action of Meas. 1—4.

MEAS. 9—16. Repeat action of Meas. 1—8, with two movements (right forward, left forward) to each measure.

Then do CHORUS.

### Part Three. (MUSIC A)

MEAS. 1. Dancers stand still, hands on hips.

MEAS. 2. Each dancer does a little jump in place, turning one quarter of the way to his left, so that partners' right elbows touch.

MEAS. 3. They stand still in this position.

MEAS. 4. They jump, making a half-turn to the right, so left elbows touch.

MEAS. 5—8. Repeat action of Meas. 1—4.

MEAS. 9—16. Repeat action of Meas. 1—8 rapidly, with two movements (jump to left, jump to right) to each measure.

Then do CHORUS.

*Part Four.* (MUSIC A)

MEAS. 1. Dancers stand still.

MEAS. 2. Number One swings his right arm vigorously, as if hitting Number Two on the left ear, and then immediately places his hands on hips. At the same moment, Number Two claps his hands together bending over slightly (making a sharp clapping noise) and then immediately places hands on hips.

MEAS. 3. Dancers stand still.

MEAS. 4. Number Two "strikes" as Number One claps.

MEAS. 5—8. Repeat action of Meas. 1—4.

MEAS. 9—16. Repeat action of Meas. 1—8 rapidly, with two movements (One strikes, Two strikes) to each measure. Do not try to place hands on hips between actions.

Then do CHORUS.

NOTE: Other traditional actions include: "pulling hair" (each boy has his right hand on his partner's head, and alternately, they pull each other forward), and "making faces" (one boy leans forward, pretending to thumb his nose at his partner, while the other leans back, with thumbs to his temples and fingers wiggling, pointing up). These are done like the other figures, alternating slowly at first, and then much faster, twice to each measure. At the end of the dance, partners shake hands vigorously and march off, arm in arm.

RECORD: Folk Dancer MH-1055-B.

## Glover's Reel

This contra dance, of recent origin, was arranged by Lawrence "Duke" Miller and stems from an old English dance which a glove cutter described to him.

**Formation:** Longways formation. Active couples (1's, 3's, 5's, etc.) cross over.

### Part One. (MUSIC A)

MEAS. 1—4. "*Do-si-do with the one below.*" The active man and lady do a "do-si-do," passing back to back with the inactive person below them.

MEAS. 5—8. "*Allemande right with your partner, and allemande left with the one below.*" The active man and lady join right hands and turn once, clockwise, with four steps. They join left hands with the same inactive person below they had done the do-si-do with, and turn once, counter-clockwise, with four steps. This must be done very quickly, to complete the action to the music.

MEAS. 1—8 (Repeated). "*Come back and swing your partner.*" Active couples swing with a buzz swing in the center, for sixteen counts.

### Part Two. (MUSIC B)

MEAS. 1—4. "*Down the center, two by two.*" Active couples walk six steps down the center of the set, and turn individually to come back on the seventh and eighth counts.

MEAS. 5—8. "*Turn, come back and cast off.*" They march up toward the head of the set, and cast off (man to the right and lady to the left) around the inactive person who had been below them. They have now progressed one place down the set.

MEAS. 1—8 (Repeated). "*Right hand star with the couple above . . . and a left hand star, back to place.*" With the same inactive couple (now above them) each active couple does a right hand star for eight steps, and a left hand star back, for eight steps. They now face the couple below them and are ready to start the dance from the beginning.

RECORD: Suggested records: "Reilly's Own," Folk Dancer MH-1072B, or "Garfield's Hornpipe," Folk Dancer MH-1065B.

# Black Nag

••••••••••••••••••••••••••••••••••••••• ENGLAND

This is one of the most popular and enjoyable of all the English country dances; its name probably derives from the English custom of giving the names of animals to inns and taverns. It has three chief parts, and each of these has two sections.

*Formation:* Longways set of three couples. All face forward, toward head of the set, lady on her partner's right.

### Part One. (MUSIC A)

MEAS. 1—4. *"Forward and back a double."* Each man holds his partner's right hand in his right. They take four light running steps forward (beginning with the right foot) and four steps backward.

MEAS. 5—8. Repeat action of Meas. 1—4.

(MUSIC B)

MEAS. 1—2. Partners face each other, joining both hands at shoulder height. The first couple slips sideward, four slide steps, toward the head of the set (to man's left).

MEAS. 3—4. Second couple slides up four steps.

MEAS. 5—6. Third couple slides up four steps.

MEAS. 7—8. All *"turn single."* Releasing hands, each dancer turns individually to his right, with four steps.

MEAS. 1—8 (Repeated). Same action is done in other direction. Third couple, then second, then first, slide down. Then all "turn single."

### Part Two. (MUSIC A)

MEAS. 1—8. *"Siding."* Partners pass each other with four steps, passing left shoulders, and return, passing right shoulders (see "Sellenger's Round," pg. 122). Repeat this action.

(MUSIC B)

MEAS. 1—2. The first man and last lady (diagonals) change places with four sliding steps, with right shoulders leading and passing back to back.

MEAS. 3—4. The first lady and last man (diagonals) do the same, with four slide steps.

MEAS. 5—6. The second man and lady do the same.

MEAS. 7—8. All "turn single."

MEAS. 1—8 (Repeated). The action of Meas. 1—8 is repeated, with dancers returning to their places in the same sequence (first man, last lady; first lady, last man; and second couple). Then all turn single.

*Part Three.* (MUSIC A)

MEAS. 1—8. *"Arm right"* and *"arm left."* Partners turn each other one with a right elbow swing, with eight steps, and do the same, with a left elbow swing.

(MUSIC B)

MEAS. 1—8. *"Men's hey."* Couple One faces down the set; couples Two and Three face up. The men do a "Shepherd's Hey," similar to the "Reel of Three" described in "Dashing White Sergeant" (pg. 154). With sixteen skipping steps they describe a figure eight. The first and second men start by veering to their left, so they pass right shoulders with each other, continuing around a large loop into the center. The third man waits for about two counts, giving the first man a chance to get by, and then starts *his* "hey," moving to the right and into the center. They end in starting positions.

MEAS. 1—8 (Repeated). *"Ladies' hey."* The ladies do exactly the same action. As they complete the figure eight, on the last two measures, the men turn single with four steps and bow to them.

RECORD: Folkraft 1174. On this record, the dance is repeated three times; each time, at the end, the first couple goes down to the foot of the set, and it is done again with each couple in a new position.

# Dances in the Square Formation

............................................ *13*

WE OFTEN THINK of square dancing as a uniquely American form of folk dance. While it is true that in the United States this is a particularly popular form of recreational dance, and that we have developed certain typical customs—such as having a caller chant directions as the dancers obey his commands—it is also true that the square, or quadrille, has a long history in other sections of the world.

The ancient Greek Pyrrhic dances, which were performed as part of the military training of young men, included some actions done in the square formation. Curt Sachs points out that a number of primitive tribes consider the square to have fertility significance, and perform certain dances in this pattern. The number of dancers in a square has ranged from four to as many as twenty-four (Catherine II of Russia performed in a quadrille for twelve couples at St. Petersburg, in 1741). But the commonest number of dancers to perform in the square formation is eight—or four couples. Playford's collection of English country dances included a number in "square for eight" formation, such as "Hunsdon House" and "Hyde Park."

The quadrille, which became popular first in France and then throughout Europe and America in the latter part of the 18th and early and middle 19th centuries, was a dance for four couples in an open square formation. Its steps were fixed and memorized, and were carefully taught and decorously performed. Usually each quadrille had five parts, each set to a separate section of music. The music itself was often borrowed from operatic or other classical sources. Some quadrilles, like the famous "Lancers," involved much bowing and scraping. Some featured many fancy steps, clogging, jigging, balletic movements and improvised actions, while others were strictly to be performed only with walking or gliding steps.

The dances described in this chapter are all traditional square dances which either descended from country dances of earlier periods, or possibly represent modifications of the quadrilles of the last century. They tend to be vigorous and rollicking, and their footwork is much like other folk dances in the book—making use of such steps as the skip, polka, buzz swing, slide and step-hop. Their patterns of movement are very much like American square dances, and it often is enlightening to a dance class to learn that the American squares and European folk dances are brothers under the skin.

## Puttjenter

•••••••••••••••••••••••••••••••••••••  GERMANY

This German square dance from the province of Westphalia shows a typical sequence of figures, punctuated by a repeated chorus.

*Formation:* Square set for four couples.

*Part One.* (MUSIC A)

MEAS. 1—8. With hands joined at shoulder height, all eight circle to the left with eight brisk walking steps. They then circle to the right and return to place, with eight walking steps.

*Chorus.* (MUSIC B)

MEAS. 1—4. All face corners. All stamp in place three times (left, right, left) and pause. All clap own hands three times, and pause. Join both hands with corner and turn once clockwise with four skipping steps.

MEAS. 5—8. Repeat action of Meas. 9—12, with *partners*.
(MUSIC C)

MEAS. 1—8. "*Ladies weave.*" Partners face each other. Men stand in place as the four ladies weave around the square with a grand right and left (giving right hands to partners, left to the next, etc.) They move clockwise, completely around the set with twelve skipping steps. They then join both hands with original partners and turn once clockwise with four skipping steps.

MEAS. 1—8 (Repeated). "*Men weave.*" As ladies stand still, the four men "weave," repeating action of Meas. 17—24.

**Part Two.** (MUSIC A)

MEAS. 1—8. Four ladies join hands in a circle and circle to the left with eight walking steps, and to right with eight steps.
Then do CHORUS.

**Part Three.** (MUSIC A)

MEAS. 1—8. Men do a right hand star, with eight walking steps clockwise. They do a left hand star with eight steps counter-clockwise.
Then do CHORUS.

**Part Four.** (MUSIC A)

MEAS. 1—8. All circle to the left and right, as in Part One.

RECORD: Folk Dancer MH-1049; Folkraft 1176; Educational Dance Recordings, FD-3.

# Cumberland Square Eight

......................................... ENGLAND

A very lively square dance, traditionally English, but also done in the United States.

**Formation:** Square for four couples.

**Part One.** (MUSIC A)

MEAS. 1—8. The head couples, in closed dance position, slide with eight steps across the set, with the *men* passing back to back. Without turning or changing position, but veering slightly, they slide with eight steps back to place, with the *ladies* passing back to back.

MEAS. 1—8 (Repeated). Side couples repeat this action.

**Part Two.** (MUSIC B)

MEAS. 1—8. The head couples form a right hand star, walk clockwise for eight steps, turn, make a left hand star, walk counter-clockwise for eight steps, and return to place.

MEAS. 1—8 (Repeated). Side couples repeat this action.

**Part Three.** (MUSIC A)

MEAS. 1—8. The head couples form a "basket." In this case, the two men join hands with each other, behind the ladies' backs. The ladies extend their hands behind and under the men's arms, and join hands with each other in front of the men. They circle to the left with sixteen buzz steps.

MEAS. 1—8 (Repeated). Side couples repeat this action.

**Part Four.** (MUSIC B)

MEAS. 1—8. All four couples join hands and circle to the left with eight light polka steps, or sixteen walks or skips.

MEAS. 1—8 (Repeated). Each couple takes promenade position and promenades around the set and back to place, with the *same* footwork.

RECORD: Folkraft 1209, 1005; World of Fun M-109-A; Educational Dance Recordings FD-2.

# La Russe

This traditional quadrille from Northern England (as performed by the Country Dance Society in the United States) is familiar to many American folk dance enthusiasts.

*Formation:* Square set for four couples.

### Part One. (MUSIC A)

MEAS. 1—2. Each man moves to the right, behind his partner, with four walking steps, to face the right-hand lady, who turns to meet him. Man One faces Lady Two, etc.

MEAS. 3—4. Each man and the facing lady do a balance or "setting" step (see "Sellenger's Round," pg. 122) to the right and to the left.

MEAS. 5—8. Each man swings this lady in closed position with eight buzz steps.

MEAS. 1—8 (Repeated). Each man walks four steps back to his partner, does the balance with her, and swings her for eight steps.

### Part Two (MUSIC B)

MEAS. 1—8. The first couple continues to swing (sixteen steps) as the others clap in rhythm.

MEAS. 1—8 (Repeated). The first couple, in promenade position, walks around the inside to the set to the right, visiting each couple in turn.

MUSIC A

MEAS. 1—4. The first and third couples (head couples) cross over, with the first couple passing between the other. They turn in place, so the lady is on the right.

MEAS. 5—8. Head couples cross back, with the third passing between, and the first outside them.

MEAS. 1—8 (Repeated). Crossover action of Meas. 1—8 is repeated.

### Part Three. (MUSIC B)

MEAS. 1—8. With hands joined in a circle, all circle to the left with eight light polka steps.

MEAS. 1—8 (Repeated). In promenade position, each couple promenades around to the right, to place, with eight light polka steps.

NOTE: The dance is repeated from the beginning, each time with a new couple active (2nd, 3rd, 4th) in Part Two. When the second couple is active, the side couples do the cross-over. When the third couple is active, the head couples cross-over, etc.

RECORD: World of Fun, M-120; Folkraft 1209.

# Man in the Hay

..................................... GERMANY

Another vigorous and enjoyable square dance, with elements of both "Cumberland Square Eight" and "Puttjenter."

*Formation:* Square set for four couples.

*Introduction:* All join hands and swing arms briskly forward and back for eight measures, while standing in place. (Music A).

### Part One. (MUSIC A)

MEAS. 1—8. With hands joined and arms swinging forward and back, all take sixteen skipping steps to the left, returning to place.

### Chorus. (MUSIC B)

MEAS. 1—2. In closed position, head couples take three slide steps to the center (to man's left, lady's right) and pause, with the man's right and lady's left foot free.

MEAS. 3—4. They take three slides back to place (to man's right, lady's left), and pause.

MEAS. 5—7. Still in closed position, head couples slide across the set with six slides, men passing back to back.

MEAS. 8. They take one more step in this direction and pause, with the weight on this leading foot.

MEAS. 5—8 (Repeated). They slide back to place, as in Meas. 5—8, with the ladies back to back.

MEAS. 1—8, and 5—8 (Repeated). Side couples repeat the action the heads have just done.

### Part Two. (MUSIC A)

MEAS. 1—8. The four ladies join hands and circle to the left with sixteen skipping steps, while the men clap.

Then do CHORUS.

### Part Three. (MUSIC A)

MEAS. 1—8. Men join hands and circle left with sixteen skipping steps, while the ladies clap.

Then do CHORUS.

**Part Four.** (MUSIC A)

MEAS. 1—8. *"Heads' basket."* The head couples meet in the center and form a basket. In this version, men join hands, raise them over the ladies' heads and lower them behind their backs to about the waist level, while ladies raise their joined hands over the men, lowering them to about the shoulder level. In this position, they take sixteen skipping steps, or quick slides, to the left, so vigorously that the ladies' feet may swing up in the air. NOTE: a buzz step may be found more comfortable, for this action.
Then do CHORUS.

**Part Five** (MUSIC A)

MEAS. 1—8. *"Sides' basket."* Side couples do action of Part Four.
Then do CHORUS.

**Part Six** (MUSIC A)

MEAS. 1—8. All circle to the left with sixteen skips, as in Part One.

RECORD: Folk Dancer MH-1051.

# *Sher*

The Sher is a Russian-Jewish square dance with figures that are like the English dance La Russe—and also like many American visiting-couple square dances. The music has a haunting, insistent quality, and the basic step throughout is a light, somewhat springy shuffle.

*Formation:* Square set for four couples.

### Part One. (MUSIC A)

MEAS. 1—8. All join hands at shoulder height, and circle left with seven steps and a stamp with the right foot on the eighth count. Circle right, seven steps, and stamp with the left.

MEAS. 1—8 (Repeated). Head couples, with inside hands joined, walk four steps forward and four steps backward to place. Side couples do the same.

(MUSIC B)

MEAS. 1—8 (Music is repeated). Head couples cross over in eight steps, with Couple One passing under an arch formed by joined hands of Couple Three. Side couples do the same, with Couple Two passing under Couple Four's arch. Now repeat the last figure, with head couples going forward and back, side couples going forward and back, heads crossing over (with Couple Three going under the arch) and sides crossing over (with Couple Four going under the arch).

### Part Two. (MUSIC C)

MEAS. 1—4. The first and second men advance three steps (left, right, left) to meet each other, almost touching right shoulders. They jump lightly on both feet on the fourth count, and then do a left-face turn, traveling to their own right around each other and, with four steps, moving toward the other man's partner.

MEAS. 5—8. The first and second men each swing the other man's partner, using a double-arm position (holding each other's upper arms, and turned slightly to left), with eight shuffling steps.

(MUSIC C)

MEAS. 1—8 (Repeated). First and second men repeat this action, advancing three steps, jumping, and turning around each other to return to their own partners in four steps, and then swinging their own partners.

The first man repeats this entire "visiting" action with the third and fourth couples. The dance is then repeated from the beginning, always with the entire Part One, and then the second, third and fourth men in turn visiting the other couples. This continues until all four men have been active.

At the end of the dance, all circle left, and then the first man winds up the others in a "rattlesnake" figure. Releasing his left hand, he leads the line under an arch formed by the fourth Couple, and to the right. The fourth man does not turn under, following the line, but lets his arms cross in front of his chest. The first man then leads the line under the arch between the third lady and fourth man, and so on, until the entire line is wound up (Diagram 49). Each set, when it has completed the "rattlesnake" action, weaves around the floor at random. It may then stop, or unwind the "rattlesnake," or go into a Hora, if the music continues.

RECORD: Columbia 20322F; Standard 8001 (Ïch Bin Deiner).

NOTE: The dance is performed to a medley of traditional melodies, and it is difficult to say that any *one* section of action fits with any *one* part of the music.

Diagram 49

# *Windmueller*

....................................... GERMANY

*Diagram 50*

Another popular German square dance, with a more complicated CHORUS figure, which makes the dance a spirited and exciting group exhibition number.

*Formation:* Square set for four couples.

*Part One.* (MUSIC A)

MEAS. 1—8 and 1—8 (Repeated). With hands joined at shoulder height, all do eight step-hops to the left, and eight to the right. The step is rather heavy and close to the floor.

*Chorus.* (MUSIC A)

MEAS. 1—8 and 1—8 (Repeated). Head couples in closed dance position, do eight step-hops (turning clockwise), moving forward and to the right, passing around each other and returning to place. The head men leave their ladies back to back with each other in the center, and quickly drop back to place. Side couples do the same, passing to the right around the head ladies in the center, and leaving *their* ladies in the center (so all four ladies stand back to back, facing their home positions, as the men drop back to place.)

(MUSIC B)

MEAS. 1—8. All four men, clapping hands, travel around the ladies to the left, with eight step-hops.

MEAS. 1—8 (Repeated). Each man holds his partner's right hand and the corner lady's left hand. With arms extended in this "windmill" formation, men do eight step-hops to their left (Diagram 50), as the ladies step-hop, turning slowly in the center.

(MUSIC C)

MEAS. 1—8 and 1—8 (Repeated). All release left hands. With a vigorous stamp and yell, each man draws his partner out of the center, into a circle, facing him. They do a grand right and left with eight step-hops (including the first heavy stamping step-hop). Partners bow and curtsey when they meet on the opposite side of the square, and then continue the grand right and left with eight more step-hops, back to home positions.

(MUSIC D)

MEAS. 1—8 and 1—8 (Repeated). Side by side, facing to right (each man has his right arm around his partner's waist, her left hand over his right shoulder), each couple walks four slow steps forward (counter-clockwise) traveling one quarter of the way around the square. In closed dance position, they do four turning step-hops, moving another quarter of the way around. This action is repeated: four walks and four step-hops, concluding the CHORUS.

### Part Two. (MUSIC A)

MEAS. 1—8 and 1—8 (Repeated). Ladies join hands and circle eight step-hops to the left and then eight to the right, as men clap.

Then do entire CHORUS.

### Part Three. (MUSIC A)

MEAS. 1—8 and 1—8 (Repeated). Men form a right-hand star and travel clockwise with eight step-hops, and then form a left-hand star and travel counter-clockwise with eight step-hops.

Then do entire CHORUS.

### Part Four. (MUSIC A)

MEAS. 1—8 and 1—8 (Repeated). Join hands in a circle with men facing center and ladies facing out. Take eight step-hops to man's left. Release left hands and partners swing around (holding right hands) so ladies face in and men face out, and continue with eight step-hops in same direction (now to man's right, lady's left). All bow or curtsey at end of dance.

NOTE: Dancers should be urged to shout (EEEE-YIIEE) during the CHORUS, particularly the "windmill" and grand right and left.

RECORD: Folk Dancer MH-1023.

## The Hatter

·············································· DENMARK

This favorite Danish quadrille is like a number of the preceding dances, and makes much use of a slow buzz step.

*Formation:* Square set for four couples.

*Part One.* (MUSIC A)

MEAS. 1—8 and 1—8 (Repeated). All join hands and do sixteen buzz steps to the left. The buzz step in this dance consists of crossing the right foot over in front of the left on the first count of each measure, and then stepping with the left foot to the side. They dip slightly on each crossing step, and lean backward to increase momentum, holding hands firmly.

*Chorus.* (MUSIC B)

MEAS. 1—2. All face partners and, releasing hands, all stamp three times (left, right, left) and pause.

MEAS. 3—4. Still facing partners, all clap own hands three times, and pause.

MEAS. 5—8. Repeat the three stamps, and three claps.

MEAS. 1—8 (Repeated). Partners stand back to back and, facing corners, repeat action of Meas. 1—8.

(MUSIC C)

MEAS. 1—8 and 1—8 (Repeated). All face partners and do a grand right and left (men going counter-clockwise, ladies clockwise) around the set, with sixteen step-hops. Partners bow and curtsey briefly when they meet on the opposite side of the set, and then continue on to home position.

*Part Two.* (MUSIC A)

MEAS. 1—8 (Repeated). Partners take closed dance position and, with right sides adjacent, swing in place with sixteen buzz steps. In this swing, each person pivots on right foot, taking longer steps with left foot.
Then do CHORUS.

*Part Three* (MUSIC A)

MEAS. 1—8 (Repeated). *"Ladies' basket."* The four ladies form a basket, joining hands behind each other's waists, and swing to the left with sixteen buzz steps.
Then do CHORUS.

*Part Four* (MUSIC A)

MEAS. 1—8 (Repeated). *"Men's basket."* The four men form a basket and do sixteen buzz steps to the left.
Then do CHORUS.

*Part Five* (MUSIC A)

MEAS. 1—8 and 1—8 (Repeated). All eight dancers form a basket and circle to the left with sixteen buzz steps. They end by leaning forward and shouting, "Hattemageren!"

RECORD: Folkraft 1160; Folk Dancer MH-1100.

# Grand Square

●●●●●●●●●●●●●●●●●●●●●●●●●●●●●●●●●●●●●●●●●●●●●● UNITED STATES

There have been many versions of the "Grand Square" in American square dancing. Here is one which has combined several traditional figures, including one from the 17th century English dance, "Hunsdon House." Once a group has learned it, it may be performed *without* calls, since the action fits the music precisely, as in an old quadrille.

*Formation:* Square set for four couples.

*Chorus.* (MUSIC A)

MEAS. 1—8. The principle of the CHORUS is that the large square is divided into four smaller squares; each person will walk around the four sides of his own small square with sixteen steps.

*"Heads advance, sides retire."* Holding inside hands, the head couples walk four steps forward to the center. Releasing each other's hand, they face each other and join inside hands with the opposite person who is next to them (lady on man's left). They back up four steps to the side of the square. Releasing hands, they face this opposite person and back away four steps along the side of the large square. They then turn to face their own partners, and walk forward four steps to meet in their home positions. (Diagram 51).

*Diagram 51*

*Meanwhile,* the side couples are doing the reverse action. They begin by facing their own partners. They back away four steps, to the corner of the large square, turn to face the opposite and walk forward four steps. Taking this person's hand, they walk four steps into the center, toward their own partners. Taking partners' hands, they back up four steps to place.

MEAS. 1—8 (Repeated). *"Sides advance, heads retire."* This action is now done in reverse. Simultaneously, the side couples walk their own small squares, beginning by going forward to the center, and the head couples begin by facing their own partners and backing away.

### Part One. (MUSIC B)

MEAS. 1—8. *"Head Ladies Chain."* The head two couples do a ladies chain (see "Portland Fancy," pg. 126) over and back, with each other.

MEAS. 1—8 (Repeated). *"Head Ladies Chain to the right."* Each head couple does the ladies chain over and back with the side couple on their right (One with Two, Three with Four).

MEAS. 1—8 and 1—8 (Repeated). *"Sides Chain."* Side two couples ladies chain over and back with each other, and then with the couples on their right.

Then do entire CHORUS.

### Part Two. (MUSIC B)

MEAS. 1—8 (*Four times*). *"Right and left through."* The head two couples do a right and left through (see Portland Fancy, pg. 126) with each other, over and back. They repeat this with the side couples on their right. Side couples then do a right and left through with each other, and with the couples on their right.

Then do entire CHORUS.

### Part Three. (MUSIC B)

MEAS. 1—8 (*Four times*). *"Half-promenade and right and left back."* Head couples, in promenade position, cross over (men passing left shoulders). They turn to face, and do a right and left through, to return to their home positions. Head couples then do this action with the side couples on their right. Side couples repeat it with each other, and then with the head couples on their right.

Then do entire CHORUS.

RECORD: Capitol 11469.

# Italian Quadrille

**..............................** FRANCE

Vyts Beliajus points out that, even though this dance is known as the Italian Quadrille, it owes its origin to France. It has a great variety of figures which may be performed in different sequences; several of the most familiar and enjoyable are described here.

*Formation:* Square set of four couples.

### Part One. (MUSIC A)

MEAS. 1—8 and 1—8 (Repeated). All join hands and walk with sixteen lively walking steps to the left, and then sixteen to the right.

### Part Two. (MUSIC B)

MEAS. 1—4. Head couples, with inside hands joined, take three steps forward, bow or curtsey, and four steps backward to place.

MEAS. 5—8. Same head couples walk forward four steps. Each man releases his partner's hand, and takes the inside hand (man's right, lady's left) of the opposite person. Turning left, he takes her back to place with him, continuing the turn so she is on his right as they face the set.

MEAS. 1—8 (Repeated). Side couples do the same; forward and back, forward and bring opposite lady back to man's place. This entire action is repeated, first with heads and then with sides, so all have original partners back.

### Part Three. (MUSIC A)

MEAS. 1—4. Men join left hands in the center, making a star, keeping inside hands joined with their partners. All walk forward six steps. Keeping the star, but releasing their partner's hand, men take two longer steps, to join inside hands with the next lady ahead.

MEAS. 5—8 and 1—8 (Repeated). Same action is done three more times, so men have original partners back.

### Part Four. (MUSIC B)

MEAS. 1—8. Still promenading with inside hands joined, the first couple leads the others into two straight lines (men facing ladies) as in a longways dance. Partners face each other and wait for end of musical phrase.

MEAS. 1—8 and 1—8 (Repeated). Men walk forward three steps, bow, and back up four steps. Ladies walk forward and curtsey, and back up. Men, and then ladies, repeat the action.

**Part Five.**

"*Reel.*" The first couple joins right hands and begins a "reel," as in the last figure of Virginia Reel (pg. 166). When they reach the third couple, the new first couple begins to reel. This continues until each couple has done the reel down to the foot of the set, taking its place there. They are now back in their original positions. The amount of music needed to perform this varies from group to group, and cannot be given exactly.

NOTE: A number of other interesting figures done as part of the Italian Quadrille are described in Vyts Beliajus' book, "*Dance and Be Merry*," Volume II.

RECORD: Harmonia H-2051-B.

# Folk Festivals and
# Special Events

..................................... *14*

*THERE ARE MANY* different types of folk dance festivals. Some may be very small, carried on by a single club or department within a school or college. Others may involve the cooperative effort of several schools, classes or ethnic groups within a community. Some festivals are regional, others state-wide and a few national in scope. A festival may be presented indoors or outdoors and may be a "single-shot" event or one that is repeated each year at the same time. It may consist solely of folk dance exhibitions, or may include mass participation in dancing as well —and may also include folk music and various kinds of pageantry and dramatic presentations.

Whatever its specific form, a folk dance festival has the following purposes:

1. It is an excellent way to build the interest of participants in folk dance classes or groups, and encouraging them to develop outstanding performance. It provides an exciting goal to shoot at and is in itself a highlight of any folk dance experience.

2. A folk dance festival serves as effective public relations, both for the sponsoring organization or group, and for folk dancing in general. In a school or college, it helps to interpret this area of the physical education or club program to other teachers, school administrators and parents. In community recreation groups, it serves to arouse interest in folk dancing and invites new participation.

Festivals were in large measure responsible for the growth of interest in folk dancing in the United States throughout the 1930's and 1940's. At various points, the Folk Festival Council of New York, the New York World's Fair, the Golden Gate Exposition in California, the annual National Folk Dance Festival, all served to bring the activity to new millions. Lucile Czarnowski has commented on the California scene:

Today, traveling through the golden state of California on a Sunday afternoon, folk music from many lands and peoples is likely to greet one's ears. Following the source of the music, dancers in gay folk costume that give an appearance of an international gathering will be found forming great concentric circles on the green lawns of parks or playing fields, or filling every foot of space in the largest city auditoriums. Dancing for all ages and for all classes has again become a favored social diversion with the Californians. . . .[6]

3. A third important aspect is that the folk festival offers an excellent means of achieving intercultural understanding. It brings forth all the most interesting and attractive elements of national and ethnic folklore and thus helps its participants and spectators achieve greater understanding and friendship. Sarah Gertrude Knott, for many years director of the National Folk Festival, has written:

. . . as together we have watched folk song and dance groups move across Festival stages, and intermingle backstage . . . we have seen prejudice give way to friendship. As we have looked beneath the merry-making surface, we have seen unmistakable evidences that people are more alike than different—a truth that so needs to be brought home to many today! We have found the same old fundamental dance patterns running through the dances of all groups, regardless of the color of the skin of the dancers, or the differences in the gay and fascinating costumes, which stamp them as belonging to a certain nationality.[7]

4. A fourth purpose of folk festivals in schools or colleges is that they serve to bring different classes or departments into closer unity, when they are called upon to work on common projects of this kind. For example, Home Economics classes can take on the job of designing and making costumes;

[6] Czarnowski, Lucile K., *Dances of Early California Days*. Palo Alto, California, Pacific Books, 1950. p. 7.
[7] Knott, Sarah Gertrude. "Let's Dance" (monthly magazine of the Folk Dance Federation of California). San Francisco, March, 1949. p. 3.

Social Studies classes can be made responsible for obtaining accurate background information pertaining to the festival theme; Physical Education classes may provide the actual performing groups; Music classes may accompany the dancers with voice or instrumental backgrounds; and Art classes can assist by providing posters, program covers, or stage decor.

### Types of Folk Festivals

What specifically are the kinds of folk festivals that can be offered?

Often, a festival will be sponsored by a single club or department within a school or college—such as an international club. At such an event, several dance demonstrations may be given by the sponsoring group, and all the spectators may be invited to join in mass dancing—with and without instruction, as needed, of folk dances. Somewhat more ambitious than this is the kind of festival in which several classes, clubs or departments may join together—some doing dances, some songs, some dramatic presentations or giving exhibits of other folk arts. Often, in the outside community, a wide variety of groups and organizations may join together, each to contribute a portion of the program, with folk dance exhibitions and other kinds of displays; at such events, there usually is the opportunity for mass dancing.

There are many kinds of themes that may be appropriate for a folk dance festival: international, historical, regional custom, holiday, etc.

The *international* theme may best be carried out by planning a United Nations or World Fellowship event. At such a festival, the dances, songs, costumes and folklore of many peoples might be displayed. Ideally, ethnic groups of various nationalities would participate. If they are not available, the plan might be to have different classes prepare exhibition dances, taking great pains to develop authentic national style, suitable costumes, etc. Occasionally, foreign students may be found at nearby colleges or universities who are skilled in their native dances and will come, either to perform or teach them, as informal ambassadors of good will.

The international theme may be provided with a story approach, in which a script is written about the "magic rug which carries the spectator around the world," or similar ideas. An announcer may then read the script, or groups of dancers may do choral speaking, to give continuity to the various dance sequences.

The *historical* theme is often appropriate, because so many folk dances have their roots deep in the past. Thus, on the Fourth of July or other important national holidays, a folk festival may celebrate America's history, by showing traditional dances as they were done at different periods in our nation's history, or by immigrant groups as they came to our shores. Somewhat similar is the historical festival which is based on the history of a particular region of the country. Several years ago, for instance, the author took part in a large festival celebrating the three hundredth anniversary of the exploration of the Hudson River Valley; dances of the American Indians, early colonists, Revolutionary and Civil War days, as well as the Gay '90's and Jazz era, were all performed.

Some regional festivals may not have this historical approach, but may be centered about a particular local industry or agricultural product, and simply bring together a number of performing groups to do dance exhibitions.

Originally, most festivals were religious in nature and were performed by primitive peoples at certain times of the year—at harvest time, time of planting, the turn of the New Year, etc. Even today, it is appropriate to have folk festivals at the time of *holidays* like Christmas, Easter, Thanksgiving and similar days. They are, of course, now removed from religious emphasis, although some of the old allegorical mummer's plays are still done in the Christmas and Spring festivals sponsored by the Country Dance Society in New York.

When a specific story is to be told, or history recounted, it may be logical to include dramatic sequences (either actors performing scenes or possibly tableaus) along with the dances. Staging such an event becomes a major operation and goes beyond the scope of folk dance festivals that most readers are probably concerned with.

In planning folk festivals, another point that should be raised is that most of the dances described in this book are either European or American in origin. This is true also in most of our schools and colleges and recreational dance groups. We are simply much more familiar with the folk culture of the European nations—and yet, if a festival is truly to have a "One World" approach, or be used to increase international or intercultural understanding, can we afford to ignore the folk dances of other lands? There is a wealth of folk material in South America, the Middle and Far East and Africa. Unfortunately, most of these folk dances (many of which are ethnic in the sense that they are more closely linked with communal custom or religion than our dances are) are quite difficult to perform. Their actions are highly stylized, their rhythms are complex and different, and they often require a high level of training for effective performance.

What is the solution?

One is—and this was suggested before—to attempt to get foreign students to perform; there *are* many thousands of such students in the United States. Another solution would be to make a real effort to locate authentic descriptions of dances of these more exotic lands. There is an excellent book of Philippine folk dances (see bibliography) and, while the dances presented are quite different from many we do in our schools, they are known to some folk dancers and can be learned without too much difficulty. Michael and

Mary Ann Herman have published directions and records for some Japanese dances, and similar sources may be discovered. It is also possible to use actual records of music of various lands (a considerable number of these are published by Folkways Records) and to *make up* dances to these. Such dances might be based on occupational movements, and might be made to resemble typical gestures of the people involved, as seen in films or photographs. While they would *not* be traditional and authentic (and this should be clearly stated) they could be an effective and colorful contribution to what would otherwise be an incomplete international festival . . .

There are a number of other problems that need to be considered in planning a festival.

These include music, decorations, publicity and promotion, costumes, acoustics, staging and refreshments.

*Music.* Although it is usually more impressive to have a live orchestra (rather than records), it is highly improbable that an orchestra can be found that can play all the different melodies of several countries in correct style and with the right kinds of instruments. The solution, therefore, is to use records, except when there is a concentration on a certain kind of dance and a properly equipped orchestra may be obtained. For instances, if many Balkan dances are to be done, a Tamburitza orchestra using the proper instruments will be highly effective. Some festival planners like to assemble all the music in advance and prepare a tape, which simplifies the problem of accompaniment. The problem of a defective tape recorder or of a tape breaking can be offset by having two machines with two identical tapes running concurrently; one machine runs with the volume turned off.

*Decorations.* Often, a folk festival is carried out on such a large scale that any attempt to decorate a large auditorium or playing field is futile. Sometimes banners may be hung, travel posters may be used, crepe paper and streamers or hay, pumpkins, or floral displays may be placed about effectively, but, in general, the amount of effort required to make a major decorative impression for a single brief event is simply not worth it.

*Publicity and Promotion.* There is no secret about how to effectively "promote" an event of this kind. It requires advance planning, much legwork, telephoning and preparing of releases, special invitations to interested groups, widespread participation of many individuals, and the use of every possible medium of publicity. It is most helpful if the event can be planned in conjunction with some other major event or happening, such as United Nations Week, Frontier Day, etc. Thus, it becomes part of that event, and the publicity is developed jointly. It is also logical to plan folk festivals as part of money-raising drives for worthwhile causes; this makes it very clear that no one individual or organization is seeking publicity for selfish ends, but rather that the Heart Fund, or some other civic enterprise, is to be benefited.

*Costumes.* Many folk dancers have their own authentic national costumes. For those who do not, it is often possible to improvise simple costumes that have the appearance of one nationality or another, with inexpensive materials and "home" sewing. About twenty of the diagrams in this book have been drawn using the costumes of different nationalities; a listing of them appears on Page 215. They may be used as the basis for planning simple costumes for folk dance exhibition purposes.

*Acoustics.* Usually, the loudspeaker system and record player that is used for folk dance classes or clubs is not adequate to handle the major demands of a large festival. When this is the case, help must be sought from the building and grounds department of the school system or college, or from any other available source. It is important to remember that, unless the dance music and announcements or script readings are heard clearly and unmuffled, enjoyment of the event is bound to be marred.

*Staging and Refreshments.* Some comment in this area has already been made, with respect to decorations. Unless the affair is quite small (in which case it is possible to do a really effective job of staging and providing authentic national foods, at a reasonable expense) it is rarely practical or rewarding to make a major effort in this area. The one exception might be in the case of a large civic fund-raising festival or similar affair in which a number of groups or organizations are participating, but in some cases not dancing or performing. Some of them might be willing to make a contribution in this area.

### Organizing the Folk Festival

In terms of step-by-step procedures for organizing a Folk Festival, it is helpful to have the classes or participating organizations that will be sponsoring the event form a Steering Committee. At the outset, this committee would:

1. Plan the time, place and theme of the Festival.
2. Extend invitations to performing groups, classes or departments.
3. Develop a timetable for future planning sessions and for rehearsals of all participating groups—including dress rehearsals.
4. Determine production costs and develop a budget.
5. Assign responsibilities to members of the Steering Committee, who will chair sub-committees dealing with:
   a. Program.

   b. Music.
   c. Decorations.
   d. Financial arrangements.
   e. Printed programs, tickets and ushers.
   f. Lighting, sound equipment and other backstage tasks.
   g. Publicity and invitations.
   h. Costumes and props.

In their book, "The Teaching of Folk Dancing," Duggan, Schlottmann and Rutledge describe three typical folk dance parties or festivals: a "Mexican Night," a "Corn Husking Bee," and an "English May Day Party." The person who is planning a Folk Festival would do well to look at these examples.

# Appendix

# Classified List
# of Dances

..............................................................

Here is a list of the dances in the book, classified according to title, nationality, formation, steps used and level of difficulty. The last classification is hard to make accurately (what is difficult for one dancer is very easy for another) but suggests how each dance might be viewed by a high school or college student with a reasonable command of folk dance skills.

| NAME OF DANCE | NATIONALITY | FORMATION | LEVEL | STEPS USED | PAGE NO. |
|---|---|---|---|---|---|
| Alexandrovsky | Russia | Couples | Moderate | Waltz, step-draw | 98 |
| Alfelder | Germany | Threes | Easy | Walk | 153 |
| All-American Promenade | United States | Couple Mixer | Easy | Walk, balance | 140 |
| Alunelul | Rumania | Circle, No partners | Moderate | Run, stamp | 87 |
| At The Inn | Germany | Couples | Moderate | Step-hop, waltz | 95 |
| Black Forest Mazurka | Germany | Couples | Moderate | Waltz, mazurka | 105 |
| Black Nag | England | Longways | Difficult | Walk, slide, skip | 183 |
| Bleking | Sweden | Couples | Children's | Bleking step, step-hop | 68 |
| Boston Two-Step | England | Couples | Moderate | Two-step, pas de bas, step-draw | 102 |
| Carrousel | Sweden | Double Circle | Children's | Slide | 58 |
| Cherkassiya | Israel | Circle, no partners | Moderate | Grapevine, step-hop | 80 |

| NAME OF DANCE | NATIONALITY | FORMATION | LEVEL | STEPS USED | PAGE NO. |
|---|---|---|---|---|---|
| Chimes of Dunkirk | France | Couple Mixer | Children's | Stamp, walk, balance | 61 |
| Circassian Circle | England | Couples | Children's | Walk, swing | 70 |
| Circle Hopak | American-Ukrainian | Couples | Easy | Stamp, leap, swing | 123 |
| Come Let Us Be Joyful | Germany | Threes | Children's | Walk, skip | 62 |
| Corrido | Mexico | Couples | Difficult | Step-draw, grapevine, soldado | 112 |
| Cotton Eyed Joe | United States | Couples | Moderate | Two-step, chug | 101 |
| Cshebogar | Hungary | Couples | Children's | Slide, skip, step-draw | 67 |
| Cumberland Square Eight | England | Square | Easy | Swing, skip, slide, polka | 188 |
| Danish Dance of Greeting | Denmark | Couples | Children's | Run, stamp | 56 |
| Dashing White Sergeant | Scotland | Threes | Difficult | Slide, pas de bas, polka | 154 |
| Doudlebska Polka | Czechoslovakia | Couple Mixer | Easy | Polka, walk | 138 |
| Eide Ratas | Estonia | Couples | Moderate | Mazurka, waltz | 108 |
| Ersko Kolo | Yugoslavia | Circle, no partners | Easy | Side-step, schottische | 85 |
| Fado Blanquita | Portugal-Brazil | Couples | Moderate | Walk, schottische, balance | 132 |
| Fireman's Dance | United States | Progressive Circle | Moderate | Ladies chain, right and left through | 128 |
| Galopede | England | Longways | Easy | Walk, skip or polka | 163 |
| Glover's Reel | United States | Longways | Moderate | Walk, swing | 182 |
| Glowworm Mixer | United States | Couple mixer | Easy | Walk | 136 |
| Grand Square | United States | Square | Difficult | Ladies chain, right and left through | 198 |
| Green Sleeves | England | Two-couple sets | Children's | Walk | 65 |
| Gustaf's Skoal | Sweden | Square | Easy | Walk, skip | 64 |
| Haymaker's Jig | United States | Longways | Moderate | Balance, swing, ladies chain | 170 |
| Hora | Israel | Circle, no partners | Easy | Side-step, step-swing | 71 |
| Hull's Victory | United States | Longways | Difficult | Walk, balance, swing, right and left through | 174 |
| I See You | Sweden | Two-couple sets | Children's | Skip | 60 |
| Italian Quadrille | France | Square | Difficult | Walk | 200 |
| Jefferson's Reel | United States | Longways | Moderate | Walk | 171 |
| Jessie Polka | United States | Couples | Moderate | Two-step | 97 |
| Jibidi, Jibida | France | Circle, no partners | Easy | Step-draw, Bleking step | 82 |
| Kalvelis | Lithuania | Couple mixer | Moderate | Polka | 144 |
| Karapyet | Russia | Couples | Difficult | Polka | 102 |

| NAME OF DANCE | NATIONALITY | FORMATION | LEVEL | STEPS USED | PAGE NO. |
|---|---|---|---|---|---|
| Kinderpolka | Germany | Couples | Children's | Step-draw, stamp | 59 |
| Klumpakojis | Lithuania | Couple mixer | Moderate | Walk, polka | 148 |
| Kohanochka | Russia | Couples | Difficult | Polka, balance | 104 |
| Korobushka | Russia | Couples | Moderate | Schottische, balance | 91 |
| Kreuz Konig | Germany | Two couple sets | Difficult | Leap, run, mazurka | 130 |
| Kuma Echa | Israel | Circle, no partners | Moderate | Schottische, run, grapevine | 86 |
| La Danza | Italy | Couples | Moderate | Walk, step-hop | 111 |
| Lady of the Lake | United States | Longways | Moderate | Balance, swing, ladies chain | 168 |
| La Raspa | Mexico | Couples | Children's | Bleking step, skip or run | 72 |
| La Russe | England | Square | Moderate | Balance, walk, swing, polka | 189 |
| Lech Lamidbar | Israel | Circle, no partners | Difficult | Leap, step-hop, balance, grapevine | 84 |
| Little Man in a Fix | Denmark | Two couple sets | Moderate | Waltz, run | 118 |
| Lott' Ist Tod | Sweden | Couples | Children's | Step-draw, slide, polka | 69 |
| Maitelitza | American-Russian | Threes | Easy | Step-swing, slide | 74 |
| Man in the Hay | Germany | Square | Moderate | Skip, slide | 190 |
| Masquerade | Denmark | Couples | Moderate | Walk, step-swing, waltz | 110 |
| Meitschi Putz di | Switzerland | Couples | Difficult | Schottische, step-hop | 92 |
| Milanovo Kolo | Yugoslavia | Circle, no partners | Moderate | Kolo step, walk | 81 |
| Minuet | France | Longways | Moderate | Minuet step, balance | 162 |
| Misirlou | Greek-American | Circle, no partners | Moderate | Grapevine, walk | 88 |
| Napoleon | Denmark | Couple Mixer | Moderate | Schottische, step-hop | 139 |
| Neapolitan Tarantella | Italy | Couples | Difficult | Pas de bas, step-hop, polka | 114 |
| Nebesko Kolo | Yugoslavia | Circle, no partners | Moderate | Two-step, balance, stamp | 79 |
| Noriu Miego | Lithuania | Two couple sets | Children's | Bleking step, walk | 74 |
| Norwegian Mountain March | Norway | Threes | Easy | Waltz or step-hop | 152 |
| Oh Susanna | United States | Couple Mixer | Children's | Walk, swing | 73 |
| Oklahoma Mixer | United States | Couple Mixer | Easy | Walk, two-step | 135 |
| Oslo Waltz | Scotch-English | Couple mixer | Moderate | Waltz, step-draw, balance | 146 |
| Oxdans | Sweden | Longways or couple (men) | Difficult | Step-draw, stamp | 179 |
| Oxford Minuet | United States | Couples | Easy | Walk, step-draw, two-step | 100 |

| NAME OF DANCE | NATIONALITY | FORMATION | LEVEL | STEPS USED | PAGE NO. |
|---|---|---|---|---|---|
| Petronella | United States | Longways | Moderate | Balance, walk, right and left through | 172 |
| Polka Zu Drien | Germany | Threes | Moderate | Polka | 160 |
| Portland Fancy | United States | Progressive Circle | Moderate | Walk, ladies chain, right and left through | 126 |
| Puttjenter | Germany | Square | Moderate | Walk, skip, stamp | 186 |
| Raksi Jaak | Estonia | Threes | Difficult | Walk, polka | 156 |
| Rig A Jig Jig | United States | Circle, no partners | Children's | Walk, skip | 63 |
| Road To The Isles | Scotland | Couples | Easy | Schottische, grapevine | 90 |
| St. Bernard's Waltz | England | Couples | Easy | Waltz, step-draw | 96 |
| Seljancica Kolo | Yugoslavia | Circle, no partners | Easy | Kolo step, balance, walk | 78 |
| Sellenger's Round | England | Couples | Moderate | Slide, balance, walk | 122 |
| Seven Jumps | Denmark | Circle, no partners | Children's | Step-hop or skip | 66 |
| Seven Steps | Germany | Couple mixer | Easy | Walk, schottische | 136 |
| Sher | Russian-Jewish | Square | Moderate | Walk, swing | 192 |
| Shoemaker's Dance | Denmark | Couples | Children's | Skip or forward polka | 56 |
| Sicilian Tarantella | Italy | Two couple sets | Moderate | Step-swing, run, skip | 120 |
| Spanish Circle Waltz | United States | Progressive circle | Moderate | Waltz, balance | 125 |
| Spinning Waltz | Finland | Couples | Easy | Waltz, step-draw | 94 |
| Sudmalinas | Latvia | Two couple sets | Moderate | Polka, waltz | 117 |
| Susan's Gavotte | United States | Couple mixer | Moderate | Walk, slide, two-step | 147 |
| Ten Pretty Girls | United States | Couple mixer | Moderate | Walk, grapevine | 141 |
| Teton Mountain Stomp | United States | Couple mixer | Easy | Step-draw, swing | 143 |
| The Bridge of Athlone | Ireland | Longways | Difficult | Two-step, sevens and threes | 178 |
| The Hatter | Denmark | Square | Moderate | Buzz step, step-hop | 196 |
| The Rifleman | England | Longways | Moderate | Polka | 164 |
| The Roberts | Scotland | Couple mixer | Easy | Step-draw, two-step | 142 |
| The Wheat | Czechoslovakia | Threes | Children's | Walk, skip | 57 |
| Three Man Schottische | United States | Threes | Easy | Walk, two-step | 158 |
| To Ting | Denmark | Couples | Easy | Waltz, walk, pivot | 93 |
| To Tur | Denmark | Couple mixer | Easy | Walk, two-step | 137 |
| Troika | Russia | Threes | Easy | Run, stamp | 151 |
| Tropanka | Bulgaria | circle no partners | Moderate | Walk, stamp, step-hop | 83 |

| NAME OF DANCE | NATIONALITY | FORMATION | LEVEL | STEPS USED | PAGE NO. |
|---|---|---|---|---|---|
| Varsouvianna | United States | Couples | Easy | Mazurka | 109 |
| Varsovienne | Sweden | Couples | Moderate | Mazurka, Waltz | 106 |
| Ve'David | Israel | Couple mixer | Easy | Walk, swing | 145 |
| Virginia Reel | United States | Longways | Easy | Walk, slide | 165 |
| Waltz Country Dance | England | Progressive Circle | Moderate | Waltz, balance | 124 |
| Waves of Tory | Ireland | Longways | Difficult | Two-step, walk, threes | 176 |
| Windmueller | Germany | Square | Difficult | Step-hop, walk | 194 |

NOTE: Many of the dances referred to as "easy" may be done by children in the elementary grades, and some of the dances referred to as "children's" are suitable for secondary school or college beginning dancers.

# Folk Dance Costumes

..............................................

It is often necessary to plan costumes for groups that will do exhibitions as part of special programs or festivals. While many adult folk dance hobbyists make a practice of *buying* elaborate and authentic costumes, this is usually too expensive a procedure for student groups. Instead, once a basic costume pattern has been chosen, it may be possible for the students themselves to make simple blouses, skirts, vests, breeches, etc., with the help of home economics teachers or parents who have sewing and clothes designing skills. As an example, one Manhasset, N.Y. junior high school class designed Dutch costumes for a folk festival conducted by the author (Diagram 52). In the words of a girl student:

We were fortunate enough to have a girl in our class who had visited Holland and had brought back an authentic girl's costume. To make the jacket, we had each girl secure a black blouse and turn the collar under . . . to get the same effect as a "dickie" we put a six inch square of printed material on top of each blouse. To make the typical Dutch hat, we had the girls experiment at home and bring in the final results. . . . we chose the best design and cut out patterns for each girl to follow. The hat was made from a sheet and when completed, was starched; the "wings" were set in hair rollers. . . . For a final touch, the girls decided to make long golden braids out of yarn, and attached them under their hats . . .

"Since the boys were unable to sew, we had to mimeograph detailed instructions and send them home . . . the buttons on their vests were circles of cardboard covered with aluminum foil . . . To make the caps, we bought painter's hats in a local store for ten cents each, sprayed them with blue paint and covered part of them with blue material . . .

To make the wooden shoes, we experimented at home again. The best method turned out to be covering old shoes with papier mache, molded to give the appearance of Dutch wooden shoes. When these hardened and dried, they were brought into class and painted yellow. . . .

*Diagram 52*

All our efforts paid off when we strolled out at the festival, hand in hand, the proudest group there!*

If a really elaborate costume of this kind cannot be made, it may be feasible to get the basic lines of the costume using old clothes that suit the purpose (as the Manhasset youngsters did to some extent) and then adding simple crepe paper sashes or vests to provide decorative accents . . .

The following diagrams, showing simple costumes of foreign lands, may be of help in this respect:

| | | | |
|---|---|---|---|
| 14. Yugoslav | 19. Mexican | 30. Danish | 39. Norwegian |
| 15. Polish | 20. Greek | 32. Italian | 45. English |
| 17. French | 28. Russian | 37. Bavarian | Dutch |
| 18. Swiss | 29. Swedish | 38. Lithuanian | |

Other useful color drawings of folk costumes may be found in the "Folk Dance Library" and the "Folk Costume Book" (see bibliography). "Viltis" has, over the years, printed many helpful photographs of folk costumes, and record stores that specialize in folk and square dance records may be able to recommend sources of ready-made folk costumes. One person who has designed and made many costumes for West Coast folk dance enthusiasts is Dorothy Godfrey, 1521 Euclid Avenue, Berkeley, California.

* Incidentally, although no Dutch dances are described in this book, two suggestions are: Old Dutch Dance (Folkraft 1194) and Dutch Couples (RCA Victor LPM 1620). Both records include instructions.

# Folk Dance Camps and Summer Schools

........................................

The following list describes a number of the camps which have been active in recent years, stating the name of the person in charge (where known) and the approximate meeting time of the year. Naturally, all are subject to change from time to time.

1. *Folk Dance Camp*, College of the Pacific, Stockton, California. Late July—early August. Prof. Lawton Harris.

2. *Rocky Mountain Folk and Square Dance Camp*, Lookout Mountain, Rt. 3, Golden, Colorado. June. Paul Kermiet.

3. *Folk Dance Camp*, Oglebay Park, Wheeling, West Virginia. End of August. Elizabeth Faris.

4. *Kentucky Dance Institute*, State College, Morehead, Kentucky. August. Naomi Durham, 4551 So. Parkway, Louisville, Kentucky.

5. *Idyllwild Folk Dance Workshop* (college credit available from University of Southern California), Idyllwild, California. July.

6. *Santa Barbara Folk Dance Conference*. August. For information, write University of California at Los Angeles Extension, Los Angeles 24, California.

7. *Lighted Lantern Folk Dance Camp*, Lookout Mountain, Rt. 3, Golden, Colorado. July. Write Mrs. Gretel Dunsing, George Williams College, Chicago 15, Illinois.

8. *Maine Folk Dance Camp*. June and late August. Write Michael and Mary Ann Herman, Folk Dance House, 108 West 16th St., New York 11, N.Y.

9. *Pinewoods Camp*, Buzzards Bay, Massachusetts. August. May Gadd, Country Dance Society of America, 55 Christopher Street, New York 14, N.Y.

# Bibliography
# of Useful Books

························································

Beliajus, Vyts: *Dance And Be Merry, Volume One.* Chicago, New York, Clayton F. Summy Co., 1940. Thirty-one folk dances, mostly from Eastern and Central Europe, with musical accompaniments.

*Dance And Be Merry, Volume Two.* Chicago, New York, Clayton F. Summy Co., 1942. Sixteen European folk dances, with musical accompaniments.

Bossing, Ed and Elsie: *Handbook of Favorite Dances.* Chicago, H. T. FitzSimons Co., 1955. Over 100 folk and round dances, with emphasis on American couple dances. Record references, some illustrations and musical accompaniments.

Burchenal, Elizabeth: *Folk Dances and Singing Games.* New York, G. Schirmer and Co., 1909. Twenty-six authentic dances of European countries, collected on the scene. Full illustrations and musical accompaniments. Other collections by Miss Burchenal: *Dances of the People,* 1913; *Folk Dances of Denmark,* 1915; *Folk Dances of Finland,* 1915; *American Country Dances,* 1918; *Folk Dances from Old Homelands,* 1922; *National Dances of Ireland,* 1925; *Folk Dances of Germany,* 1938.

Czarnowski, Lucile: *Dances of Early California Days.* Palo Alto, California, Pacific books, 1950. Scholarly collection of forty traditional dances showing Spanish influence, with fine historical backgrounds, music and diagrams.

Duggan, Anne, Schlottmann, Jeanette, and Rutledge, Abbie: *The Folk Dance Library.* New York, Ronald Press, 1948. Fully detailed descriptions of eighty-three folk dances, with illustrations, music, maps, national folklore, teaching guides, etc., in five volumes: *Folk Dances of the United States and Mexico; Folk Dances of the British Isles; Folk Dances of Scandinavia; Folk Dances of European Countries;* and *The Teaching of Folk Dance.*

Haire, Frances H.: *Folk Costume Book.* New York, A. S. Barnes, 1926. Descriptions and colored illustrations of twenty-six national folk costumes. Out of print, but might be found in college or community libraries.

Hamilton, Frank (editor): *American Round Dancing.* Temple City, California, Windsor Record Co., 1953. Discussion of present-day American round dancing, with teaching guides and step analysis. No dances are presented.

Harris, Jane, Pittman, Anne and Waller, Marlys: *Dance A While.* Minneapolis, Minn., Burgess Publishing Co., 1950. Varied collection of recreational dances, including eighty-nine folk and round dances and mixers. Comprehensive teaching guides and excellent dance descriptions. Record references.

Herman, Michael: *Folk Dances for All.* New York, Barnes and Noble, Inc., 1947. Nineteen popular folk dances with illustrations, music and record references.

*Folk Dance Syllabus.* New York, Folk Dance House, 1953. Descriptions of seventy-two folk dances taught at the Hermans' Maine Folk Dance Camp, with record references, folklore anecdotes and recipes for national dishes.

Holden, Rickey: *The Contra Dance Book.* Newark, New Jersey, American Squares (Dance Record Center), 1956. Detailed presentation of over 100 American line and progressive circle dances, with historical information and teaching guides.

Hunt, Paul, and Underwood, Charlotte: *Calico Rounds.* New York, Harper and Bros., 1955. Useful teaching guides and record references for forty-nine folk and round dances, with emphasis on American rounds.

Kaltman, Frank and Kulbitsky, Olga: *Teachers' Dance Handbook.* Newark, New Jersey, Bluebird Publishing Co. (Dance Record Center), 1959. Extremely thorough presentation of folk dancing and singing games in the elementary grades, with step analysis, teaching guides, diagrams, music and record references for 116 dances.

Kennedy, Douglas: *England's Dances: Folk Dancing Today and Yesterday.* London, G. Bell and Sons, Ltd., 1950. Fascinating analysis of English folk dancing, past and present, showing its relation to American forms and its function as community and personal expression. Does not include dances, but provides excellent background reading on specific dance types.

Kirkell, Miriam and Schaffnit, Irma: *Partners All—Places All.* New York, E. P. Dutton Co., 1949. Forty-four American and European dances and singing games, with music and record references.

Kraus, Richard: *Square Dances of Today.* New York, Ronald Press, 1950. Fifty-five dances, mostly square, with a number of useful American singing games and couple dances. Helpful teaching and calling guides, with illustrations, music and record references. Other books on recreation leadership by Kraus, with large sections of square and folk dances and singing games: *Play Activities for Boys and Girls,* McGraw-Hill Book Co., 1957; and *Recreation Leader's Handbook,* McGraw-Hill Book Co., 1955.

Lapson, Dvora: *Dances of the Jewish People.* New York, Jewish Education Committee, 1954. Good descriptions of a variety of European Jewish and Israeli dances, with music and record references.

La Salle, Dorothy: *Rhythms and Dances for Elementary Schools.* New York, Ronald Press, 1951. Graded collection of fifty-eight European and American folk dances and singing games, plus creative rhythms, for elementary schools.

Lawson, Joan: *European Folk Dance, Its National and Musical Characteristics.* London, Sir Isaac Pitman and Sons, Ltd., 1953. The most comprehensive and scholarly treatment of European folk dancing available. Only a few dances are described; this is primarily a background text.

Rohrbough, Lynn: *Handy Play Party Book.* Delaware, Ohio, Cooperative Recreation Service, 1940. Best source of traditional American singing games and play parties, plus some European folk dances (over 110 dances in all) with music.

Shaw, Lloyd: *The Round Dance Book.* Caldwell, Idaho, Caxton Printers, Ltd., 1948. Authoritative study of traditional American round dances, with thorough step analysis and invaluable background information for about 125 dances.

Tolentino, Francisco Reyes: *Philippine National Dances.* New York, Chicago, San Francisco, Silver Burdett Co., 1946. Excellent descriptions of over thirty folk dances of the Philippines, with cultural backgrounds, diagrams, photographs and music.

The best folk dance magazine to have been published during the past fifteen years has been "Viltis," edited by Vyts Beliajus. Its current mailing address is: Box 1226, Denver 1, Colorado.

# Sources for Folk Dance Records

••••••••••••••••••••••••••••••••••••••••••••••

The Folk Shop, 161 Turk Street, San Francisco 2, California.

Dance Record Center (also handles books), 1159 Broad Street, Newark 2, New Jersey.

Folk Dance House, 108 West 16th Street, New York 11, New York.

Berliner Music Shop, 154 Fourth Avenue, New York, New York.

P. A. Kennedy Co., Ltd., Box 816, Brandon, Manitoba, Canada.

The address of Educational Dance Recordings, Inc., which has made four albums of folk dance records based on the dances in this book, is P.O. Box 6062, Bridgeport, Connecticut. The author supervised the recording sessions and prepared the instructional materials for these records and, naturally, recommends them for use. They include the following dances:

FOLK DANCE FUNFEST: F.D. 1. Kinderpolka, Greensleeves, La Raspa, Chimes of Dunkirk, Carrousel, Circassian Circle, Norwegian Mountain March, Gustaf's Skoal, Noriu Miego, Come Let Us Be Joyful, Cshebogar and I See You.

DANCING 'ROUND THE WORLD: F. D. 2, Jessie Polka, To Ting, Napoleon, Seven Steps, Maitelitza, Cumberland Square Eight, Masquerade, Hora, Doudlebska Polka, Troika, Seljancica Kolo and Road to the Isles.

FOLK DANCE FESTIVAL: F. D. 3. St. Bernard's Waltz, Misirlou, Oklahoma Mixer, Cotton Eyed Joe, Sellenger's Round, Eide Ratas, Portland Fancy, Cherkassiya, Kalvelis, Mexican Waltz, Korobushka and Puttjenter.

DANCES OF MANY LANDS: F. D. 4. Karapyet, Varsovienne, Kohanochka, Nebesko Kolo, Sicilian Tarantella, Spanish Waltz, Little Man In A Fix, Fado Blanquita, Kuma Echa, Meitschi Putz Di, Fireman's Dance and Dashing White Sergeant.

These records may be ordered directly from David McKay Co., Inc., 119 W. 40th St., New York 18, N.Y.